Successful
MOONLIGHTING TECHNIQUES
That Can
MAKE YOU RICH

OTHER BOOKS BY FORREST H. FRANTZ, SR.:

The Miracle Success System:
   A Scientific Way to Get What You Want Out of Life

Parametrics:
   New Key to Successful Take-Charge Management

Successful
MOONLIGHTING
TECHNIQUES
That Can
MAKE YOU RICH

by
Forrest H. Frantz, Sr.

Parker Publishing Company, Inc.   West Nyack N.Y.

Second Printing.....November, 1970

PRINTED IN THE UNITED STATES OF AMERICA
13–863423–8   B & P

THE AMAZING WORLD OF
THE MOONLIGHT ENTREPRENEUR

*Of 50 executives making more than $20,000
a year in their regular jobs—
70% moonlighted in fields ranging from
services to complex investments—
20% wished they could moonlight but didn't
know how.*

The amazing world of the moonlight entrepreneur is peopled by men and women who refuse to accept the status quo in life. They voice their protest—not with marches and riots and loud voices, but through constructive action that leads them on to fortune, independence, security and the optimum conditions for happiness in life. The life of the moonlight entrepreneur is exciting because in each venture he undertakes, he pits his wits against the world. The competition in the world of business is fierce, the stakes are large. The moonlight entrepreneur senses this excitement as he pursues large gains from small investments and ultimate complete financial independence. Yet, the moonlight entrepreneur does this without any risk whatsoever. Why? It's simple. He maintains a full-time job which provides the basic economic support for his family. His moonlight enterprises help to build his estate. If one of his moonlight ventures is less than successful, he simply regroups and tries another. Nothing is lost.

You'll never get very rich just by working for somebody else. The very best you can expect to do is to live comfortably and retire in reasonable circumstances at the age of 65. On the other hand, if, during your working years, you set aside a portion of your income for investment and a portion of your spare time for management of your investment, working years will be shortened considerably. You'll retire at 45, 40, or perhaps even before the age of 30. And, of course, when I speak of retirement, I speak of being able to do whatever you want to do for the rest of your life.

This book is your handbook for building and controlling a million-dollar business empire from scratch in four to seven years. It shows you the techniques of top money-makers who have moved from poverty to riches, from moderate income to fortunes, and from drab existence to luxurious living. You'll learn how to apply these techniques to build your bank account, expand your holdings, increase your influence, and command the respect that accrues to the wealthy and successful.

This book is a hard-hitting handbook for money-making with step-by-step techniques to guide you all of the way. I have personally used the techniques that are communicated in this book or have learned of them from people who I know have used them successfully. Hence there's no make-believe theory. You have an army of successful, wealthy men and women at your side telling you exactly what to do, guiding you over every obstacle, and answering all the questions that arise along the way. This book will help you lay your plans, exploit your resources to the hilt, obtain financing where it's needed (bigger loans than you ever dreamed possible), and let you in on the secrets of getting a venture off the ground and making it succeed immediately.

The methods and techniques presented here are easy to apply. Two to three hours a day can sometimes stretch as small an investment as a $20 bill into $10,000 in a matter of months. As a matter of fact, in Chapter 1 you'll discover methods for starting from zero and building a $20,000-a-year income. Every day smart money-makers negotiate deals that bring them income for the rest of their lives. They often do it in an hour or two using the methods that this book puts at your fingertips.

The ways to wealth and fortune are numerous. I've tried to present them so that confusion is avoided and methodical analysis of the various possibilities is made easier. In the first chapter, you start to set up your fortune-building business immediately. In the second chapter, you look at a number of methods that can be employed in turning a very small investment into a reasonably large nest egg. You will be off to a good start by the time you reach Chapter 3 and learn some of the ways in which big deals are made. By the time you have the scientific principles for, no-risk fortune building of Chapter 4 under your belt, you'll be ready to investigate in Chapter 5 the eight ways in which all fortunes are made and then apply the secrets of profitable trading that are presented in Chapter 6. In Chapters 7 through 10, you'll explore hundreds of individual ways in which fortunes have and will be made; then in Chapter 11 you get ready for your bigger leap. You learn how to organize, finance, and operate bigger profit ventures—how to set up a corporation. In Chapter 12, you'll read actual case histories showing how others have built and controlled business empires. You'll tune in on actual million-dollar business plans. You will see how checkpoints were met, how losses were countered. You'll be able to apply the same foolproof techniques in your own quest for wealth.

I could wish you luck, but that would be ridiculous. Luck sometimes plays a part, but not very often. What you read in this book and what you do about it will give you a million-to-one edge over the guy who merely counts on luck.

Forrest H. Frantz, Sr.

CONTENTS

3. THE KICKERS—GOVERNMENT LOANS AND SUB-
SIDIES, DISCOUNTS, INTERLOCKING DEALS,
MULTIPLE PROFITS, AND OTHER BUSINESS
ACCELERATORS (Continued)

4. SCIENTIFIC PRINCIPLES FOR NO-RISK FORTUNE
BUILDING 73

4. SCIENTIFIC PRINCIPLES FOR NO-RISK FORTUNE
   BUILDING (Continued)

5. TAP THE EIGHT PRINCIPAL WAYS IN WHICH
   ALL FORTUNES HAVE BEEN AND WILL BE
   MADE 87

6. THE SECRETS OF PROFITABLE TRADING . . 105

6. THE SECRETS OF PROFITABLE TRADING (Continued)

7. DISCOVER YOUR RESOURCES: THE SECRETS OF CONVERTING JUNK, FREE RESOURCES, AND UN-RECOGNIZED CAPABILITIES INTO VALUABLE ASSETS 123

7. DISCOVER YOUR RESOURCES: THE SECRETS
OF CONVERTING JUNK, FREE RESOURCES,
AND UNRECOGNIZED CAPABILITIES INTO
VALUABLE ASSETS (Continued)

8. HOW TO MAKE OUT IN MANUFACTURING
AND CONSTRUCTION   145

8. HOW TO MAKE OUT IN MANUFACTURING AND
   CONSTRUCTION (Continued)

9. HOW TO MAKE A KILLING IN SERVICES . . .   161

10. LEASE, RENT, SELL AND "CREATE" YOUR
    WAY TO UNTOLD WEALTH   177

1

HOW TO START—15 EASY STEPS
THAT YOU CAN TAKE THIS WEEK

STEP 1: ORGANIZE AND FINANCE

The form that your organization will take depends on the kind of business involved. Generally speaking, an entrepreneur operates as a proprietor. He may own all or most of the equity in one or more corporations, syndicates, and joint ventures. Some individuals operate all of their business under a corporate structure. In getting started as a moonlight millionaire, it is hardly essential that you set up a corporation to start. As you develop your business activities you may want to put some of them into a corporate structure. But until your net income starts to get quite large, there's no particular tax advantage in the corporate structure. The other advantage that a corporate structure affords is limited liability. Since limited liability contains the responsibility of the corporation, you'll frequently be asked to set up contracts on a personal basis as an individual in deals where your corporate liability is inadequate.

In the event that you're going to enter a business venture with someone else in addition to yourself, it is usually wise to set up a corporate structure. Although we can't get into the details of forming a corporation in this chapter, we will treat this extensively in Chapter 11.

There are two basic ways to finance your business. You will, in any event, provide some of the capital from your savings or your other earnings. If additional capital is required, you can secure it either through equity financing or debt financing. Equity financing is characterized by a venture investment on the part of another person. In return for this venture capital, you give the other person part of your business. They benefit in the profits according to the percentage of the business that they own. In debt financing you borrow from the bank or some other lending institution and secure the debt with a mortgage or some other form of collateral. If you have a substantial financial position, you can borrow money on your signature.

It is usually desirable to build your business with 100 percent ownership at the outset. Hence, you wring out the problems in the business, go through the difficulties of starting up, and take the business up to a point where you know how it operates and where you're ready to expand it intelligently. At this point, your past performance places you in a position to sell equity in your business more advantageously. Then you're in a position to sell less equity at a greater price.

Of course, if you choose to take in one or more other persons, your business may have some very valuable benefits accruing to it. First of all, if the people that you take in have special expertise that augments your own, it may help your business to grow faster. The capital that is invested by persons that you take into your business also places it into a position to grow faster.

See Chapter 2 for the secrets of getting started with little or no capital.

STEP 2: PRACTICE DETAILED PAPER PLANNING AND ANALYSIS TO INSURE PROFITABILITY

Your business venture is more likely to succeed if it is based on good planning. Start by making a list of the things that have to be done to get your business started; then after you've made this list, use it to develop a second list which shows what has to be done in chronological order. Lay this plan out with respect to time based on the amount of time that you're going to put in your business. Next, determine the amount of money that will be required in each step of your plan.

The next piece of planning paper that you need is an anticipated estimate of the revenue that your business will receive. Lay this out either on a weekly or a monthly basis. This will give you some kind of feel for the amount of money that you can expect to take in. When you've done this, you need to lay out a cash flow projection. A typical cash flow projection is shown in Figure 1. Start by entering the revenue indicated by your revenue plan. Then develop the costs that are involved in the conduct and the production of the business revenue that you've projected. Wherever you come up with a positive cash flow at the end of the week or month, you have cash that you can carry

	Period 1	Period 2	Period —
1. Total Income			
2. Purchases			
3. Gross Profit $(1 - 2)$			
4. Rent			
5. Utilities			
6. Phone			
7. Advertising			
8. Office Supplies			
9. Salaries and Wages			
10. Other Overhead			
11. Overhead (sum 4 thru 10)			
12. Net Profit (loss) $(3 - 11)$			
13. Cash (14 preceding period)			
14. Current Cash (need) $(12 + 13)$			

Figure 1. Cash Flow Projection

forward for the conduct of your business. Whenever you come up with a negative cash flow, it is essential that you have funds available to cover the deficit. You can do this either by arranging for loans in advance to cover these anticipated deficits or you can readjust your schedule by injecting economies in some of the preceding months that will even out the cash flow. You may go through four of five cash flow projections before you come up with a suitable overall plan. Nevertheless, this is the only way that you can assure yourself of the greatest probability of profitability and success.

STEP 3: ESTABLISH A BROAD PLAN FOR PROFIT

Set up your broad plan of profit before you step in and begin to purchase haphazardly. Determine the business that you're going to get into, how you're going to extract revenues in the performance of the business, where you're going to obtain the resources that you'll use in your business, the kind of capital equipment that you need and have, and where you're going to locate your business. Figure 2 is a form suitable for jogging your mind and helping you to think through these various aspects in your broad plan for profit.

PROFIT PLAN MIND JOGGER

1. Type of activity or business: _____.
2. Starting date: _____.
3. The hours of the day that I'll be able to work at it: _____.
4. Provisions for staffing the business during times I can't work at it (if this is necessary): _____.
5. Capital required: _____.
6. How I'll raise the capital: _____.
7. Type of space and building I'll need including consideration of location requirement: _____.
8. Equipment I'll need: _____.
9. Manpower and skills I'll need: _____.

10. Sources of supply I'll need: —————————————————.
11. How I'll sell my products or services: —————————————

    ——————————————————————.
12. How I'll fill requirements 7 thru 10: —————————————

    ——————————————————————.
13. Sales, costs, overhead and profits by months for a year: ———————

    ——————————————————————.
14. Possible surprise costs, setbacks, and contingencies that I should
    be prepared for: ————————————————————

    ——————————————————————.
15. Licensing, tax, insurance, utility, telephone, and other items that
    enter into overhead and/or affect profit ——————————

    ——————————————————————.

Figure 2. Profit Plan Mind Jogger

STEP 4: SET UP AN EFFICIENT LOW COST OFFICE

Your hip-pocket will do, but an office is better. You don't
need an office for effect; you need an office as a money-making
facility. Your office should be a place where you can get away
from interruptions, but a place from which you can communicate with all the world. It should be a place where those with
whom you do business can find you and meet with you. It should
be the center of your business activity. From it you should be
able to reach out to all the world and make inquiries. Around the
periphery of your office, you should have the basic books, texts
and references that you'll use in determining the strategies for
the conduct of your business. You should also have available the
information that enters into the daily detail of your business. I
have such an office. It's approximately 12 feet by 20. Through
this office, I ran close to $100,000 in gross moonlight business in
1968. This office is located in my home, and that's where you
should locate yours. Since you're moonlighting, you don't want
to waste time going to and from your office.

Consider these possible places on your residential property as
a location for your office:

1. A bedroom
2. The basement or cellar
3. The garage
4. An outbuilding
5. Your kitchen

Joseph Cossman began his mail-order empire on his kitchen table. I hardly recommend this as a start because you've always got to pull things up and put them away. If you're going to start to build a business empire, you need a place where you can leave your work, go to your full-time job, and come back and pick up where you left off the evening before. That's why I feel that you need a place apart from the rest of your household life.

STEP 5: EQUIP YOUR OFFICE

You'll need a phone in your office for communication. An extension on your personal phone will do for a start. Eventually you'll want your own private line.

You'll need a desk, filing cabinets and file folders. You can get the desk and filing cabinets at a used office supply house, at a used furniture store, or at a salvage house. Get more filing capacity than you think you'll need at the outset, because as you build your information files, you'll find that you need considerably more than you have. All in all, for even the most modest start on your office, you're going to be looking at an investment of approximately $100 if you don't already have some of this equipment.

Bookshelves are another important item. The controller of business empires is guided by information. He obtains his information from books, magazines, newspapers, and his personal contacts.

Your office should be well lit, and it should be heated and air conditioned. If you normally live without these luxuries, then you can live without them in your office. But if you're used to them, you'd better have them in your office. There's nothing more conducive to success than a comfortable environment. Carry this idea through in decorating your environment, too. You don't need $500 drapes, but $10 worth of curtains can do wonders for your office atmosphere.

Now let's get down to other facilities. In the event that you decide to manufacture your way to wealth, you'll need a production facility. Very often your garage will serve the purpose. If your garage is inadequate, there are other possibilities. A neighbor may have a garage he is willing to rent. Or keep your eye open for buildings around town which are for rent or lease. Approach the owner or the agent to rent these buildings on a temporary basis at a reduced rate till he can find a long-term tenant. Bear in mind that location is usually unimportant for a manufacturing facility. Hence you can consider out-of-the-way, low-rent areas for your factory. But, if you take a temporary facility at a reduced rate, bear in mind that there are costs involved in moving, and plan accordingly. Be sure to specify a 30-day notice so you can make orderly move plans. (Actually, if a building has been vacant for a long time, there's not too much danger of the owner finding a new, high-rent paying tenant in a hurry.)

If the nature of your business demands a downtown office, there are many alternatives open. Ruth Behrens operates a suite of offices in the Union Fidelity Life Building in Dallas. Ruth provides secretarial services to the men who have offices there. The men pay a fixed rental fee and Ruth and her associates answer the telephones, provide secretarial services, and afford a very effective front for all the men who occupy the individual offices in her suite. Similar arrangements ranging from office to desk space in bullpen type offices are available in most cities in the United States.

STEP 6: BUILD INTELLIGENCE FILES AND A SOURCE LIBRARY

The builder of enterprises bases his actions on information and the intelligent assessment of that information. Right at the outset of your entry into business enterprise, set up information files and a source library. You can set them up by products, disciplines, types of business or any other logical system that appeals to you. I suggest the following periodicals to any entrepreneur who is looking for a rich financial future:

1. *The Wall Street Journal.* This publication stays abreast of the major business news in the United States. No matter how local your business may be, it is important that you stay abreast of national news pertaining to business. Furthermore, this publication is a key to knowledge of the movement of the national stock markets as well as the over-the-counter markets. Although you may not invest in stocks, you will find it wise to be knowledgeable of the activity in the market. It frequently is the bell-ringer to other economic developments.

2. Your regional newspaper. Your regional newspaper gives you an insight into the activities of the major business leaders in the key city in your region. Peruse it daily with particular attention to real estate, financial news, and the classified ads. You'll be surprised at the number of opportunities for contact and for doing business that will develop. (Incidentally, you can make a fortune just buying, selling, and trading through the classifieds in a big city.)

3. Your local newspaper. Assuming that you don't live in a large city, you're probably located in a community that has a local newspaper. You need to stay abreast of this in order to develop your local contacts and have an assessment of opportunities that are available in your hometown.

4. *Fortune* magazine. This magazine, published by Time, Inc., is a source of statistical as well as biographical and report-

ing information on the state of business in the United States. It gives you a feel and a flair for business activity throughout the United States and abroad. If the price of the subscription seems too high, peruse this periodical each month at your public library.

5. *Forbes.* One of the leading publications in the financial world keeps you abreast of other developments in the business world.

6. *Business Week.* A McGraw-Hill publication, it reports in detail on activities in the business scene. A weekly, it provides information on a more timely basis than the monthly and bi-weekly publications.

7. *Dun's Review. Dun's Review,* another business publication, provides different treatment on some of the business subjects that you'll encounter in the other publications. Published by Dun & Bradstreet.

8. *Nation's Business.* This magazine, published by the Chamber of Commerce of the United States, provides another perspective on the world of business.

9. The American Management Association fills an important role in the business world. It is a centroid to which all aspects of big business gravitate. I heartily recommend membership in the American Management Association to anyone with big business aspirations. Members of the AMA receive *Management Review* on a monthly basis. This periodical reviews and digests new books and also articles in other publications. It also contains a number of feature articles. Members of AMA also receive on a six-issue-a-year basis the publication, *Personnel.* Upon joining AMA, you designate a major and a minor field of interest. You receive additional publications pertaining to these two fields.

10. One of the major sources of information for your business intelligence files is the Superintendent of Documents of the United States. The Office of the Superintendent of Documents, Government Printing Office, Washington, D.C. 20402, publishes

the *Statistical Abstract of the United States* annually. This is a base publication which provides statistical information that has cost millions of dollars to compile. From it you can develop marketing trends and statistics concerning every aspect of American life and business as well as an assessment of international values. The *Abstract* is just one of many publications available from this source. I heartily recommend that you get on the mailing list of this agency. The following publications are brief catalogs of selected publications available from the Government Printing Office:

> *Selected Publications Available Through*
> *Your Local United States Department of*
> *Commerce Field Office.*   (Free)

> *A Survey of Federal Government Publications*
> *of Interest to Small Business.*   (45¢)

Get this book, too:

> *Information Please Almanac, Atlas and*
> *Yearbook.*   New York, Simon and Schuster.

It's an annual full of data and useful information that's handy in business pursuits.

Here's another useful reference:

> Coman, E. T., *Sources of Business Information.*
> Los Angeles, University of California Press, 1964.

This reference lists books and periodicals of business value.

I use a relatively simple filing system. I file things and information by subject matter, and of course, I file my correspondence by the name of the correspondent. My correspondence file is small; my intelligence file is large.

Here's another thought on building your information and intelligence files. Any U.S. corporation of any size at all will be pleased to furnish you with an annual report. All you have to do is request it of the corporation's Public Relations Department, and you'll receive an annual report by return mail.

STEP 7: BUILD A LIST OF CONSULTANTS

There are other sources of information besides publications. These sources of information are human beings—people like you and me. We, in turn, are valuable sources of information for others. Your friend, the lawyer, can provide you with a number of ideas about business and about the law. Your friend, the engineer, may have an idea that you can turn into a profitable product. Your friend who works at the bank can give you more ideas about finance than you can generate in many hours. Your friend, the retailer, may save you the loss of a fortune through what he can tell you about his own business. Recently I had an opportunity to buy a restaurant. Before I made the move and acquired the property, I talked to one of my friends who owns and operates a restaurant. I learned that he was operating the restaurant only because he couldn't find a qualified renter—one who could operate profitably and pay the rent. That made me decide not to buy the restaurant since I didn't want to get into the operation myself. A quick telephone call saved $200,000.

Of course, there's lots of information and counsel that you can receive free from the U.S. Government, from your state government, and from your local government. And don't forget the Chamber of Commerce—local and national. Your state government provides information through its various agencies. To get a better feel for the counsel that is available to you through your state agencies, contact your local representative in the state government. To obtain local information, take time out and make a visit to City Hall. You'll come back loaded with maps and various other forms of information that will be quite valuable to you. To gather information at the Chamber of Commerce, go to the Research Department. They'll have industrial site information, marketing information, information about educational institutions in the area, and a number of other things. You'll be amazed at what you'll learn.

Other sources of information are trade associations. Check your local library for compendiums of trade associations to find specific associations that deal in the business areas that are of interest to you.

And since we mentioned the library, let's say a little more about it. Your public library contains books that are valued in hundreds of thousands, and perhaps millions, of dollars. They're all there—yours to use free. All you have to do is get up the energy to go down to the library and take a look at them. Learn how to use the card indexes to find your information in a hurry. Your public library can be exceedingly valuable to you.

It's a good idea to build a file of consultants—people in various lines of business, local, state, and national governments, Chambers of Commerce, associations, and other organizations to whom you can turn for information. Remember, it's a two-way street. You ought to give as well as get.

STEP 8: ESTABLISH SIMPLE RECORDS THAT DO BIG, COMPLEX JOBS

You've got to keep adequate records in order to be able to measure the success of your business, for income tax purposes, and in order to know how much cash you have and where you can apply it. Without adequate records, you can hardly expect any great success, and you can't possibly expect to know what you are doing in your business.

Overly complex records, on the other hand, will cause you to waste time and may provide you with information that is almost as useless as none at all. Records, to be useful, must be easy to keep and must tell the pertinent facts of your business at a glance.

I keep records of the checks I write in my check register. I attribute cash and checks which I receive to the source, on my deposit slips. This is easy to do in my venture since I don't receive much cash and I rarely ever receive checks smaller than $100. I give receipts (from a receipt book) whenever I receive cash. (If you're in a business that involves a lot of small cash sales, you'll do well to use a sales book.) Hence, my personal activity in making record keeping entries is minimal. My accountant constructs a set of more detailed books from my check registers, deposit slips, and bank statements. We use these for income tax purposes and to analyze results.

Some of my income is from businesses managed by others. For these I have weekly summary forms (Figures 3a and 3b) which list receipts, cash expenditures, and bank deposits. I write the checks to pay large bills myself. Some of my managers disburse only small cash amounts to cover petty expenses. All of my managers make bank deposits. The bank sends copies of the deposit slips to me. This arrangement provides reasonable control.

I keep my business activities separated by using separate business checking accounts in different banks. This simplifies my bookkeeping somewhat, although it requires that I keep five times the minimum checking account balance that I'd have to keep with only one account. The advantages outweigh the disadvantages in my case.

STEP 9: ESTABLISH A CHECKING ACCOUNT

Set up a checking account for your business in order to simplify your record keeping and your handling of transactions. Your bank will have checks imprinted with the name of your business at nominal cost. If you do the kind of business which requires you to make check payments out of your pocket at various locations, I suggest that you get the small pocket-type checkbook. I use these extensively in my business operations because I need the mobility they afford. On the other hand, if you operate in a manner that permits you to write all of your

Weekly Report — Zodiac Apartments

Saturday ＿＿＿＿＿＿ to Friday ＿＿＿＿＿

(Break up Partial Weeks at Beginning and End of Month)

Apt. No.	Date	Amount	Dep. Date
101			
102			
103			
104			
105			
106			
107			
108			
109			
110			
111			
201			
202			
203			
204			
205			
206			
207			
208			
209			
210			
211			
Total			

BANK DEPOSITS

	Date	Amount
1.		
2.		
3.		
4.		
5.		
6.		
7.		
Total		

VACANCY RECORD

Apt.	From	To	Days Vacant
Total			

PETTY CASH DISBURSEMENTS

	Date	Amount	To	For
1.				
2.				
3.				
4.				
5.				
6.				
7.				
8.				
9.				
10.				
Total				

Service Calls

Other Matters

Figure 3a. Apartment Weekly Report Form

30

Frantz Retail Operations Report

From ____ to ____, 19__. Account _____ Reporter _____

	M	T	W	T	Etc. →
1. Register: Present					
2.　　　　　－ Previous					
3.　　　Sales & Sales Tax					
4.　　　+ Misc. Income					
5.　　　Gross Revenue					
6.　　　－ Sales Tax					
7.　　　Gross Rev. to Res.					
Paid Out (cash)					
8. Food					
9. Supplies					
10. Misc.					
11.　　　Subtotal					
12.　Deposits					
13.　　　Subtotal					
14.　　　+ Short － Long					
15.　　　Total: Line 5					
Bank					
16. Previous Balance					
17. + Deposits: Line 12					
18.　　　Subtotal 16 & 17					
Check Paid Out					
19. Food					
20. Supplies					
21. Labor (Net)					
22.　　　Subtotal 19 + 20 + 21					
Line 18 － Line 22 =					
Current Bank Balance					

Figure 3b. Retail Operations Weekly Report Form

31

checks in your office, one of the large checkbooks is more desirable.

STEP 10: OBTAIN LICENSES AND PERMITS

States, counties, and cities require licenses of anyone who engages in selling. Check your local laws to be sure that you comply with them.

If you're going into a business which involves a service such as plumbing or electrical contracting, you'll need the necessary permits or licenses that your city requires. Most cities require a license to practice in such trades. In addition, most cities require that you obtain a building permit for each specific job.

You can get a feel for the licenses and permits that will be required in your business by talking to someone who is engaged in a similar business. You can also get official information on these subjects from your local, state, county, and city tax offices.

STEP 11: NAME YOUR BUSINESS

By the time you've finished this book, you'll have made up your mind about the kind of business you're going into. At this point, you'll want to select a name, and possibly a logo, to use on your stationery and promotional material.

STEP 12: GET YOUR PRINTED MATERIALS

When you start your business, it is probable that you will need calling cards, letterheads, and envelopes. You may also need billing forms, purchase order forms, scheduling forms, and perhaps some others depending on the kind of business that you are entering.

When you order printed materials, remember this: The printer will give you a better deal if you have your mind made up before you walk in. So here's what I suggest. Set up the name of your company and develop the logo before you ever walk into the printer's office. Shop by phone before you place your printing order. Perhaps you can find a moonlight printer who will provide you with printed materials at considerably less money than the union printers. The whole point is: Make up your mind as to what you want. Then shop around a little and you'll cut costs considerably on your printing.

Don't overlook the possibility of arranging barter on any material that you'll need to get started, including printed material. For example, if your hobby is electronics, you may be able to arrange to swap some television set repair for your printing. By bartering services, you can minimize the cash cost of your business start-up.

STEP 13: AFFILIATE AND PUBLICIZE

Membership in your Chamber of Commerce, business and professional organizations, and civic clubs will help you by providing valuable personal associations. You can overdo it and spend all your time attending meetings. But, if you're going to be active in business, you should be active in business and professional organizations related to your endeavors, and you should serve your community through civic organizations. Organization dues are deductible.

Publicize your entry into business through the local press and by the other means cited in Chapter 10, part of which deals with publicity, advertising, and selling.

Give your financial statement to your bank, your local credit agencies, and Dun and Bradstreet. This will clear the way for open account buying and borrowing. Even if your net worth isn't big, it's worth doing. As your net worth grows, it will be a matter of record in the places where it counts.

If you hire people, you have social security and tax matters to tend to. Your accountant can help you on this.

STEP 14: ACCUMULATE CAPITAL EQUIPMENT

The capital equipment that you need in your business doesn't necessarily have to be the newest and latest. If you're going to operate a small manufacturing venture, you may be able to use some tools that you already own. Used tools and machines may be obtained from a number of sources at considerably less than the cost of new tools and equipment. Check your telephone directory under the appropriate classifications, such as "Used Equipment," "Salvage Yards," "Wrecking Yards." Also check the classified sections of city newspapers and trade periodicals in your field of endeavor.

Another way to accumulate capital equipment that you need at low cost is to advertise for it. Frequently you will come across some real buys in this way.

If your requirement for capital equipment involves a substantial amount of money, check with your banker. It is probable that you can get a loan with the equipment as collateral. If you made good buys, your banker may provide financing for up to 80 or 90 percent of the cost of the equipment.

You can get the equipment that you will need by renting or leasing. Generally speaking, renting or leasing is more expensive in the long run than purchasing the equipment because the lessor makes a profit for his services. For equipment that will only be used occasionally, rental by the day or week may be considerably less expensive than outright purchase. But, if you use the equipment on a daily basis, buy it if you can.

In the event that you are buying new equipment (and you can sometimes work this on used equipment) ask the seller to give you a 90-day open account. If you can work this arrangement without any interest charge or penalty, you can make arrangements with your bank to pick up the financing of the equipment at the end of 90 days; hence you have 90 days use of the money interest-free, and the equipment can be earning the necessary difference required for the "down payment."

STEP 15: BUILD YOUR STAFF

In the operation of your business, you may require the services of others on professional, skilled, and unskilled levels. If you're off to a small start, you don't want the responsibility of a regular payroll that you have to meet regardless of the fortunes of the business. You want to be able to hire your talent and your manpower when and as you need it. I suggest that you use other moonlighters in your business. A small, inexpensive classified ad in the "Help Wanted" section of your local newspaper under "Part-Time Work" or a similar classification should get you plenty of responses. In your ad indicate the kind of work that you want to have done, that it is part-time, and that the work schedule is flexible. This kind of detail will usually weed out nonqualified responses, and tend to get you the kind of people that you most need for your activity.

When you get telephone responses to your ad, get the information on the individual that is shown in the form Figure 4. If the individual sounds qualified, tell him the rates that you anticipate paying, and give him other details pertinent to the job. Determine then if the individual will fit into your scheme of things. Don't commit too quickly to people on employment because you may find that you get later inquiries from people who are more qualified than some of your early ones.

Whenever you can, try to gear your payment arrangements to productivity. Hence, if you're getting into a small manufacturing venture, try to set your rates up on a piecework basis. Or if you are getting into a sales venture, try to set up the compensation of your salesmen on a commission basis. This way you pay only for results, and you have an automatic incentive for the people that you employ.

Name:
Address:
Phone Number:

EXPERIENCE:

Type of Work	Employer	From	To

WORK DESIRED:

TIMES AVAILABLE:

TELEPHONE IMPRESSION:

APPOINTMENT FOR PERSONAL INTERVIEW:

Figure 4. Telephone Interview Form

BUSINESS STARTER CHECKLIST

1. Set up an efficient office in which to study, think, and work. It should be quiet with a pleasant working atmosphere.

2. Equip your office with telephone, desk, file cabinets, bookshelves, and chairs. A typewriter, an adding machine, and possibly a copying machine or duplicator may be useful in your office.

3. Build intelligence files and a source library.

4. Build a list of consultants—friends you'll turn to for information and advice in various specialty fields.

5. Establish a record-keeping system that is simple, but effective. Your accountant can advise you in this regard.

6. Establish a business checking account.

7. Obtain the necessary licenses and permits.

8. Decide how you're going to make your fortune. Select a name and logo (trademark) for your business.

9. Obtain stationery and other printed forms.

10. Affiliate and publicize.

11. Establish a broad plan for profit.

12. Accumulate the necessary capital equipment for your business. Stick to used equipment where possible, and use loan leverage to acquire it.

13. Build your staff.

14. Organize and finance your venture.

15. Practice detailed paper planning, review and analysis.

2

100 WAYS TO TURN $100 OR LESS INTO $10,000 FAST

This chapter title might just as well have been HOW YOU CAN GET STARTED WITH LITTLE OR NO CAPITAL. For example, you'll learn of several possible business enterprises that you can start with absolutely no capital at all. You'll learn of others which you can start using resources and materials that you already have on hand without any additional cash investment; and you'll learn of some that require only $5, $10, or $20 to get started. Nevertheless, the success of any venture depends greatly on adequate financial backing. It is for this reason that I chose the $100 as a recommended starting point for even the most modest venture. You'll learn before you have gone more than two pages further that $100 is adequate leverage in some instances to develop borrowing power of $10,000.

THE SECRETS OF FORTUNE BUILDING

The biggest secret of fortune building is one that is hardly apparent when you study the great fortune builders. To find this greatest secret of all for building fortunes, one must study those who have not built fortunes. If you question a man who hasn't made the grade, he'll usually blame it on luck or fortune, or he'll say that money doesn't matter to him and that other things in life are more important. Yet I'm sure that every person in this world would truly love to be free of money worries and that a little more of the material things in life would lead to greater individual happiness.

So what's the secret. Why is it that more people are not fortune builders? The answer? It's a relatively simple one: They don't know how! Mark this as your first secret for fortune building:

> To build a fortune, you must first learn
> how to do it.

"How to Build a Fortune" is what this book is all about. I'm not going to waste a lot of time trying to get you all pumped out to go out and make a fortune. You've probably made the decision already. If you haven't, you at least have the desire or you wouldn't be reading this book.

Another secret of fortune building that has been used by many fortune builders is the technique that makes it possible for the man or woman with financial and family responsibilities to build a fortune without risk. It's moonlighting. Your full-time job provides sustenance and support for your family. Your part-time activities, then, can be concentrated on fortune building without this diversion. The fortune builder who quits his job and launches full-time into the matter of fortune building usually has acquired a considerable amount of capital before he starts. Other things being equal, if two men start on a job at the same time, and one of them begins to build his moonlight fortune while the other accumulates his money to eventually start a business, the moonlighter will be able to leave his job and devote full-time to a going business long before the saver has built his nest egg and is able to launch his business activities. Furthermore, while the other man is simply saving, the moonlighter will be acquiring considerable business experience.

$100 LEVERAGE CAN GET YOU A $10,000 LOAN

One of the most powerful tools of the entrepreneur is leverage. Leverage works like this: Suppose you have $100 in cash to start. You want to buy a property that costs $10,000. You might proceed as follows: You negotiate with the owner of the property to buy it for $1,000 down, so you need an additional $900. You go to your bank and arrange for a $900 loan. This plus your $100 in cash gives you the necessary $1,000 down. Dismiss the idea that the $900 loan might be hard to get. You'll get the "how-to" in Chapters 3, 4, and 11.

Suppose the seller wants all cash. You might go to your bank or mortgage company and indicate that you'd like to buy this property; you want them to provide a $9,900 loan. Chances are you'll have a difficult time setting it up. The lender will want to have the property appraised. Then, if you're willing to pay on an amortized payment basis, that is, equal payments, over the period of the loan, the lender will generally be glad to lend you 80 percent of the appraised value. Assume that the property appraises for $12,000. The lender will be willing to lend you $9,600. Hence you'd need another $300 in addition to your $100. You can usually obtain this through a loan from a relative or a friend. Another possible source is a separate personal short-term loan, secured by other collateral such as stock, chattels, or furniture. But, the easiest place of all to get this is on a second lien mortgage secured note to the seller! Sure he wants cash, but he'll extend $300 credit to get $9,700!

Frequently, property for sale has existing low interest financing. If the unpaid debt on the property is large, say for example on our $10,000 property there is an existing debt of $7,500, you should try to get the seller to take a second lien note on the property. The seller may still want you to have at least 10 percent of the value of the property in cash. In that case, you'll still have to rustle up that $900. There are plenty of ways to do this, and we'll cover them in detail later.

Vast fortunes have been made by purchasing property and then leasing or renting it. The high leverage possibilities, the net cash flow (sometimes referred to as "spendable" income), the automatic debt amortizing of the property, the inherent collateral value of the property, appreciation, inflation, and the tax cancellation (shelter) aspect of allowed depreciation make improved property investment outstanding.

Moonlight Fortune Tip (MFT) 1
Include rent-lease properties in your Moonlight Fortune Ventures.

You'll get the full treatment and plenty of practical knowledge on this subject in Chapter 10. I learned a lot of this the hard way growing from one rental unit to 35 rental units in a year.

The main point of this section is: Smart money people use leverage to accelerate growth and make bigger profits. If you use $100 and make a 50 percent profit in a month, you have $150 at the end of the month. If you borrow $900 (now you have $1000) and make 50 percent, you have $1500 minus $900, or nearly $600 after paying interest, that's all yours! You made $450 with borrowed money!

Put MFT 2 in your book and use it in every turn of your business career. Moonlight Fortune Tip 2 makes top money for top money makers. Chapters 4 and 5 will fill your mind with powerful applications and techniques associated with this and other basic fortune expansion principles.

Moonlight Fortune Tip (MFT) 2
Employ loan leverage to increase your working resources, and hence your volume of business and profit.

Remember, we're talking about borrowing for investment and business purposes. *Never, never,* borrow for non-income producing purposes—unless to fulfill a true need and to keep available cash free for investment. And that brings up another point that we may as well get across right now.

You want to build a fortune and have the good things in life. To do it, you progress in two precisely related steps. First, you build your fortune; second, you have the good things in life. In other words, you live a conservative economic life to free capital for financial investment and growth. If you don't, you slow the fortune growth process.

One of my friends, controller for an electronics company, in 1965 was driving an old, beat-up (probably 1953) car. Most people at his station in life wouldn't have been seen dead in the old trap. At the time, his company's stock was selling at 8. His frugality with his car had freed enough cash and commanded enough leverage to allow him to add $10,000 worth of his company's stock to his holdings. The stock is better than 60 now, so he made about $75,000 by driving that old car. (Incidentally, he bought that new dream car in 1967.)

> *Moonlight Fortune Tip (MFT) 3*
> Make your fortune first. Then enjoy the
> finer material things in life.

In Chapter 7, you'll uncover numerous ways to increase the resources at your command for building your fortune. But one of the fundamental ways is to invest everything now and spend lavishly later.

HOW TO TRADE $100 INTO $10,000 CAPITAL IN ONE YEAR OR LESS

O. L. Nelms, Dallas investor and businessman, is probably worth more than $10,000,000 today. He began his career while he was in grade school, trading pocket knives and other things. In more recent years, he's been trading real estate. Joe Carlson, about whom we'll say more in this chapter, started trading automobiles while he was in college and has been quite successful at it. Actually, trading is a part of every form of business venture. The trader may deal in properties, in stocks and bonds, in furniture, in antiques, in artifacts, art, coins, stamps, books, contracts, notes, automobiles, trucks, freight cars, or airplanes, to mention only a few of the multitudinous possibilities. The trader may engage in barter—that is, trade item for item, or trade item for item plus cash boot, or he may buy with cash and sell for cash. Hence, the wholesaler and the retailer are really traders in the truest sense.

Now let's look at the mechanics of turning $100 into $10,000 capital in a year or less. First of all, we'll take the case which involves simple cash turnover without employing any loan leverage. Assume that you and your wife are going to get into the business of trading antiques and artifacts. You take a Saturday afternoon and start to hit the stores and shops and invest your $100 in what you consider to be good buys. You take your purchases home, clean them up, and prepare them for sale. During the next week your wife makes some telephone calls while you are at work, and you make some in the evening. You might place an ad in the classified; and during the course of the first week, you sell the items that you purchased for $200. You won't sell them all at once, and your wife will do some shopping during the week to replenish your stock as the items are sold. But for purposes of simple analysis, we'll assume the investment is made and that everything is sold out at the end of the week, and that the money is again reinvested at that time. We'll assume that the maximum sales that you can make in the course of a month are $1600. The table at the top of the facing page shows how your money—your net worth—grows.

You'll notice that at the end of the 12th month, you will have $6400 in cash plus an inventory that cost you $3200 and has a resale value of $6400. This example is a simplified one to put the idea and the principle across. You would obviously be reinvesting your money as quickly as it is free and, consequently, you could be turning it on a much faster basis. It is also probable that

MONTH	PURCHASES	SALES
1	$ 100	$ 200
	200	400
	400	800
2	800	1600
3 & 4	1600	3200
5, 6, 7, & 8	3200	6400
9, 10, 11, 12	6400	6400 plus an inventory that will sell for $6,400.

you could increase your sales beyond the $1600-a-month level since, as your capital becomes large, you will invest in higher cost items. Consequently, you might make single sales of $1,000 after the fifth month, whereas your largest single sale during your first month will probably be approximately $100.

Now, let's assume that you use leverage in building your antique and artifact business. You might do this by purchasing your initial inventory for 10 percent down; hence, you would have a $1,000 inventory to start and you would only have $100 in cash invested. Your dealings then might progress as shown in the table below. We are assuming here that you can make sales of up to $4000 per month since you are dealing in higher priced merchandise.

MONTH	EQUITY	PURCHASES	SALES
1	$ 100	$1,000	$ 2,000
2	1,100	2,000	4,000
3 & 4	3,100	3,100	6,200
5, 6, & 7	6,200	6,200	12,400

Notice that during the first month, you leverage your $100 cash equity position into a $1,000 purchase. This gives you the capability of $2,000 in sales. In the second month, you purchase $2,000 of merchandise after paying off the $900 in debt that you incurred the first month. Hence, you have $1,100 in cash toward your second month's $2,000 purchase. You sell this for $4,000, and after paying off the $900 that you owe on this merchandise, you have $3,100 to begin with in your third month. For purposes of simplicity, I've assumed that you operate on cash from this point out.

Doug P. is an electronics technician in the aerospace industry. In 1964, he began to service television sets in his garage on an after-hours basis. Color had started to move in, and a lot of black and white sets were being put out of service. Doug took the sets on trade-in and purchased others for cash. He fixed them up. Then he placed classified ads in the newspapers advertising used black and white TV sets at low, low prices. His response was tremendous, and his black and white set trading venture netted him $3,500 profit the first year. Doug still has his job with the aerospace company. But he also owns a downtown TV sales and service business that clears $15,000 a year for him.

Trading is an art that deserves full book treatment. I've only been able to allocate one chapter to the subject in this book. Consequently, in Chapter 6, you'll get a fast course in big-time trading secrets that successful traders will rarely divulge to anyone.

One point that I hope you've discovered in this section is:

> *Moonlight Fortune Tip (MFT) 4*
> To accelerate fortune building, apply turn-over pyramiding.

Turnover pyramiding is the method that permits you to make your resources grow from $20 or $100 to $10,000 in less than one year's time.

HOW CARLSON MAKES $6,000 A YEAR AFTER HOURS

Joe Carlson started to sell automobiles in his spare time to pay his way through college. He was rather successful at it and he continued to sell automobiles in his spare time after he graduated and took a job as an engineer. He buys automobiles from dealers at wholesale prices, cleans them up, makes minor repairs and then resells them for profits ranging from $50 to $300 per automobile. He works in conjunction with a small body shop and garage. When Joe sells the car, he pays off the bill that he incurred on the car.

Joe does his selling at the place where he works for the most part. He advertises on the swap bulletin board, and the word gets around from satisfied customers to new prospects. He also uses his social contacts in his church, PTA, and Lions Club. He makes about $6,000 a year on an after-hour effort that averages about 15 hours per week.

There is a lesson in the experiences of Joe Carlson and Doug P. that is worth noting. There was nothing very sexy or big-dealish in what they did. But, they founded their businesses on a fundamental essential to business success. And, here it is:

> *Moonlight Fortune Tip (MFT) 5*
> To build investment return or accelerate sales and profits, go where the action is: select products and investments that tap demand.

There's no point in getting into a business that isn't in demand. A Chevrolet dealership would go great, but you wouldn't expect much from a wagon dealership, would you? Yet, every year thousands of people start low-demand businesses. Go where the action is: tap existing demands.

TWENTY TYPICAL HOBBIES THAT CAN TURN $100 INTO $10,000 IN A YEAR

Hobbies frequently afford rich opportunities in business. Manual skills and home arts, frequently the basis of hobbies, can be transformed into businesses. Specialized knowledge of specific products and objects of value, such as that acquired in the pursuit of collection hobbies can also be transformed into income pursuits. Even reading, as uncommercial sounding a pursuit as one can imagine, has profit possibilities. Here's a list of twenty typical hobbies that can be transformed into profitable moonlighting businesses:

Carpentry	Art
Decorating	Knitting
Quilting	Pets
Sheet metal work	Electronics
Chemistry	Writing
Photography	Flowers and gardens
Farming	Antique collecting
Stamp collecting	Coin collecting
Gadgeteering	Inventing
Reading	Model building

If your hobby is carpentry, you might profit on it by building special cabinets or furniture. The amateur artist can capitalize on his hobby by offering his paintings for sale in a gallery, through dealers, and directly to individuals, or by accepting commissions to paint portraits or other pictures. The hobbyist decorator can sell his or her decorating capabilities. The decorator generally works with suppliers and collects a percentage from the supplier (10 percent seems to be common) for all sales resulting from the decorator's recommendations. Women who enjoy knitting and quilting can command high prices for their handmade products. While they'll hardly get rich selling these products, they can utilize the profits from this activity to invest in other ventures. Animal enthusiasts can get into the pet or pet-grooming business. Hobbyists with interest in sheet metal work, electronics, and chemistry can start manufacturing, consulting, and service businesses. The writer can sell his output to magazines and newspapers and to book publishers. He can even take a flier and do his own publishing. The photographer can tap the same markets that are open to the writer, and can, in addition, do portrait and special occasion photography. Those with interest in flowers and gardens can provide yard and garden services and have an open road to a complete nursery business. If your hobby is farming, you might invest in a farm or consider the possibility of leasing a farm.

The collector, whether his specialty be in antiques, stamps, coins, artifacts, old automobiles, or what have you, can trade in his specialty and can serve as a consultant in his specialty. If he can make repairs to the objects peculiar to his collecting hobbies, this offers an additional business opportunity. The gadgeteer can frequently sell his services to others and can market his own gadgets. The inventor can sell manufacturing rights (licenses) to manufacturers or can manufacture his own products. He also can trade his inventions or rights to his inventions for equity positions in businesses. The person who enjoys reading can start a research service or can perform abstracting services. Businesses frequently require literature and library research. The specialist offering this service would be much in demand.

The collecting hobbies have always been popular as a diversion, but during the past two decades, they have also become popular as a hedge against inflation. Hence, many collectors are investors rather than hobbyists.

$20,000 A YEAR—SPARE TIME—NO INVESTMENT REQUIRED

An income of $20,000 per year in your spare time without any investment is a realistic and attainable goal. The people who are doing it number in the tens of thousands. I'm speaking about opportunities in spare-time selling. You may, on first thought, envision the door-to-door salesman, who receives more "no's" then "yes's" and ends up with a few $2.00 sales at the end of the day. If you do, readjust your thinking for a moment and open your mind.

The successful part-time big-money salesman operates in a manner characterized by one or more of the following methods:

1. He begins as a door-to-door salesman and recruits additional salesmen. He eventually ends up with a pyramided sales organization.

2. He has a universal product that appeals to a broad array of prospects.

3. He has a product that has repeat sales potential.

4. He has a unique product that appeals to a special kind of prospect. He spends a considerable amount of time obtaining qualified prospects and hence minimizes wasted sales calls.

5. He selects a product whose price, when multiplied by the number of sales that can be made in a given unit of time, is relatively large.

Chapter 10 explores other facets of the selling business, exposing the opportunities and detailed "how-to" approaches for starting and prospering in them. Chapter 10 gets into the detailed "how-to" aspects of advertising, publicity, and sales that have turned many a $100-a-week man into a $50,000 a year enterpriser. Franchises offer sales opportunities, too. I'll treat this subject in Chapters 9 and 10.

To get quick exposure to a host of selling opportunities, get copies of these magazines:

Specialty Salesman
307 N. Michigan Ave.
Chicago, Illinois   60601

Salesman's Opportunity
850 N. Dearborn St.
Chicago, Illinois   60610

TYPICAL WAYS TO START A MANUFACTURING ENTERPRISE

Many of the nation's large businesses were started as part-time ventures. And even more of the nation's small manufacturing businesses (less than 500 employees) were started as part-time businesses. Eventually most of these businesses will become big business. Many of these manufacturing enterprises had their start in a garage, a workshop, a spare room in the house, or even in the family kitchen.

Ole Evinrude started his motor manufacturing enterprise in his spare time. He was working as a pattern maker, and during the course of a Sunday afternoon picnic, he hit upon the idea of the outboard motor. He traded pattern-making work to get the parts for his motor made. He built a prototype, tested it on a boat, and it was an immediate hit with everyone who saw it. One of his friends borrowed his motor over the weekend and came back the following Monday with cash orders for ten of the motors. This was the beginning of the Evinrude Outboard Motor business.

Dr. Thomas D. Welch started the Welch Grape Juice enterprise in his kitchen. He was communion steward at his church in Vineland, New Jersey. His stand against liquor was staunch, and he looked for a wine substitute. In the process, he tried to get juice out of raisins, he worked on blackberries, and finally on Concord grapes. He was successful with the grapes and put up a dozen bottles for his church. He accelerated his kitchen factory and was soon selling to other congregations. Then he moved his enterprise into his barn and started turning out Welch's Grape Juice in 100-quart batches.

In the two cases just cited, manufacturing businesses were started with small outlays of capital. Many manufacturing businesses are started each year from equally humble beginnings. The resourceful moonlighter uses available space in his garage or outbuildings, his basement or elsewhere in his home as a starting point for his manufacturing activities. He utilizes tools and equipment that are part of his household effects or a part of his home workshop to get started. The equipment that he needs but doesn't have is frequently bought in used condition at a fraction of the original price. He uses leverage by making small down payments on the equipment that he acquires. In some instances, he rents his equipment instead of buying it. Some men get into the manufacturing business by subcontracting their manufacturing work to established businesses that are equipped to produce components, subassemblies, or even the end product.

Building construction is another form of manufacturing. In this case the builder, who is the manufacturer, takes his manufacturing capability out to the building site and erects a structure on a piece of ground. The builder usually employs subcontractors to perform portions of the job of raising the structure and equipping it with services and facilities.

In Chapter 8, we'll deal with getting started in manufacturing and construction. There you'll learn how to discover or develop a product to manufacture, how to develop your sources of raw materials, how to get production started, how to price your product, how to market it, and the other details of making money in the manufacturing business.

Meanwhile, you may want to order some books on the subject which are available at low cost from the government. Order them from the U.S. Government Printing Office, Washington, D.C. 20402.

> *Management Aids for Small Manufacturers,* Annuals 4, 5, 6, 7, 8, 9, 10, 11, 12, and 13. (These Annuals cost from 35 to 45 cents each, and they're well worth the money.)
>
> *Starting and Managing a Small Building Business* (35¢)

MONEY-MAKING SERVICES

The service industry is growing faster than any other segment of the American business scene. It is growing faster than manufacturing, mining, agriculture, and construction. During the past twenty years, service man-hours have grown approximately 150 percent, whereas manufacturing man-hours have grown only by about 20 percent. The small growth in manufacturing man-hours is due in part to the continuing development of machines and automation. Services defy automation and new services have been developing at a rapid rate. The challenge of conceiving and developing new and better services is one of the brightest horizons open to the idea-generating entrepreneur.

Of course, the professional services (doctors, lawyers, dentists, accountants, consulting organizations, scientific laboratories) have always been big income earners. But it isn't essential that you engage in these long-education, big skill services in order to earn top money. For example, John Scully formed a company called Everything For Everybody. He set his business up in Greenwich Village in 1966. Within six months, he had taken on close to 600 projects, including finding interpreters, feeding pets, selling pets, balancing checkbooks, taking pets for walks, finding acts for entertainments, finding a harpsichord repairman, and numerous other services.

Other entrepreneurs and investors have taken less offbeat flings in the service field. Here are just a few services that are always in common demand: Laundries, dry-cleaning shops, beauty and barber shops, linen supply houses, diaper services, photo studios, shoe repair shops, funeral services, clothing alterations, fur repair and storage, Turkish baths, reducing salons, costume and dress-suit rental agencies, rug and furniture cleaning establishments, coin-operated service machine establishments, and checkroom concessions. As a million-dollar moonlighter, you may engage directly in any of these businesses, or you might simply invest in them. One of my friends owns half-interest in each of two beauty shops. His original investment was approximately $5,000. He earns about $1,000 a month from his investment in these ventures. It takes very little of his time, and it is extremely profitable.

But that only scratches the surface of the fortunes available to the alert entrepreneur in the services field. In Chapter 9, we'll discuss a host of other services in this field, and the miscellaneous business-services fields in the device-maintenance and repair-services fields to mention only a few. You'll learn how to set your business up, how to establish your prices and rates, and you'll be introduced to the government's "Starting and Managing" publications which deal with specific service businesses.

OTHER WAYS TO BUILD YOUR FORTUNE

There are many other ways that you can start traversing the road to moonlight wealth with no investment or a very small investment. Many fortunes have been built in natural resources. You'll learn more about the techniques for investment and fortune building in this field in Chapter 7. New ideas, inventions, and new technologies form the foundation of many business and investment successes. Arthur Rock built a fortune from a small investment by recognizing up-and-coming technological companies early in their business history. Chapter 10 addresses the subject of profiting on technology, creativity, and the hidden wealth in your mind.

Leasing and renting is a business that is not confined to real estate. Automotive equipment, industrial equipment, tools, and even human beings, to mention just a few, are resources that are rented at large profits by an increasing number of businesses. Cash preservation, uneven demands, and direct expensing are some of the facets of the business and income-tax world that have fostered the rapid growth of the leasing and renting business. In Chapter 10, you'll learn the six basic characteristics of money-making rental products and a host of leasing "why's and how's" that will put you in a position to start your own leasing and renting business.

Many fortunes are made in the world of finance. In Chapter 11, you'll learn how to organize, finance, and operate big-profit ventures. You'll learn how to form a corporation and how corporations and joint ventures are profitably financed. You'll learn how to get favorable debt financing with limited resources.

Once you've got your business started, you can make it grow most rapidly if you apply the money-making secrets of the big-time operators. In Chapter 4, you'll build your background knowledge of kickers, government loans and subsidies, discounts, interlocking deals, multiple profits, and other business accelerators. In Chapter 5, you'll be introduced to a host of scientific principles for no-risk fortune building. No matter what business or investment venture you enter, the information in these two chapters will become a major part of your day-to-day operations.

Now, let's get on to the next chapter and learn about the mechanisms that will help you in your quest for a fortune.

3

THE KICKERS—
GOVERNMENT LOANS AND SUBSIDIES,
DISCOUNTS, INTERLOCKING DEALS,
MULTIPLE PROFITS, AND OTHER
BUSINESS ACCELERATORS

THE KICKERS HELP YOU BUILD FORTUNES FAST

The astute businessman looks for the kickers. The kickers help you build fortunes fast. They oftentimes enable you to do the seemingly impossible. Kickers come in many forms. Sometimes they're government subsidies. Kickers appear on a daily basis as discounts, interlocking deals, multiple profits, and in numerous other forms. The "kicker" is the item that makes a deal more profitable and more attractive. In many cases, the kicker provides the final element that makes the deal come off or makes it become profitable. Just today, for example, I was talking to a friend who purchased a 200-acre farm. He had some difficulty getting the loan to make the purchase. He tied the purchase of an insurance policy in as a kicker, and he obtained the loan from the insurance company.

THE GOVERNMENT IS A GREAT BIG HELPER

The government is a great big helper to anyone who has the initiative to build a business or to make an economic, social, or moral contribution to the American public. The Federal government helps through subsidies, loans, and loan guarantees. It helps by giving counsel and by disseminating information through its various agencies and the U.S. Government Printing Office. State governments help the moonlight enterpriser by providing advice, information, and in some cases, loans and subsidies. Local governments frequently provide help for new industries by purchasing land, erecting factories, and then leasing them to new industries at extremely attractive rates. Sometimes local governments grant tax exemptions to new businesses which move into the locality.

There are more helps available from the various governments than any one individual can readily uncover and utilize. In this chapter, I'll touch on just a few of the available helps. An in-depth treatment of available government assistance would require several volumes. The government is a great big helper, and the astute moonlight enterpriser utilizes this help whenever he can.

HOW TO CASH IN ON A MULTIPLICITY OF
GOVERNMENT LOAN ASSISTS

The United States Government is a source of loans and loan guarantees. A Federal loan guarantee will sometimes be the kicker that jars a big bank loan loose for you. The million-dollar moonlighter can take advantage of these loans and guarantees in developing his business and his investments.

The Small Business Administration has a loan program expressly designed to assist small businesses, including manufacturers, wholesalers, retailers, service establishments, and other small businesses that are independently owned and operated. These loans are made to small business companies to finance construction, convert, or expand. They are granted for the purchase of equipment, facilities, machinery, supplies, or materials, and to provide working capital.

To qualify, the applicant must have good character and must be able to show evidence of managerial and business skill. He must have enough capital in the business so that when the Small Business Administration loan is added, it is possible to operate the business on a sound financial basis. The past record and future prospects of the business must show sufficient probable future income to provide reasonable assurance of repayment. The loan must be adequately secured by real estate, chattel mortgages, or other suitable collateral.

Small Business Administration (SBA) loans will not be authorized to pay creditors when such payment would not solve the pressing long-term financial problems of the business. SBA loans are not granted solely to effect a change in ownership of a business, except in very special circumstances. They are not granted to provide capital to a company that is primarily engaged in lending and investment activities, in newspaper and magazine publication, or in radio and television broadcasting. Nor are SBA loans granted to companies that derive a substantial part of their income from the sale of alcoholic beverages or from gambling activities. A loan will not be granted where it would encourage monopoly or be inconsistent with the American system of free competitive enterprise. SBA loans will not be granted for moving a business in order to avoid obligations incurred in the location from which the business is moving; nor will a loan be granted to move a business from a labor surplus area or from a locality where the move would cause serious unemployment.

The types of regular business loans that the SBA administers are:

1. Bank participation loans.
2. SBA guaranteed bank loans.
3. Direct loans.

Bank participation loans have been slowed down in recent years due to tight government funds resulting from Vietnam war costs. So have direct SBA loans. As of early 1969, direct loans were impossible and participating loans were limited. However, SBA was guaranteeing business loans and this activity isn't likely to be interrupted. The situation may have changed since this book has gone to press. Check on it if you're interested.

The maximum that SBA will guarantee for a single borrower is $350,000. Working capital loans have a 6-year maturity while portions of the loan allocated to construction have a maximum 15-year maturity. These same limits and terms apply to direct and participating loans when funds are available.

To obtain further information and application forms, write to:

Small Business Administration
Washington, D.C. 20416

or contact your nearest SBA field office.

SBA has additional loan programs. These include:

Simplified Bank Participation Plan
Simplified Early Maturity Plan
Economic Opportunity Loans
State Development Company Loans
Local Development Company Loans
Small Business Investment Company Loans
Physical Disaster Loans
Economic Injury Loans

For further information, obtain SBA form OPI-7.

OTHER GOVERNMENT LOAN ASSISTS

The departments of Defense, Interior, Agriculture, and Commerce, as well as GSA, AEC, and NASA, will guarantee loans for defense production. Apply at your bank. They'll apply in turn through a Federal Reserve Bank to the appropriate government department or agency.

The Maritime Administration will insure loans for financing ship construction or reconditioning. For information write:

Maritime Administration
Washington, D.C. 20235

Agricultural loans can be secured from a broad array of Federal agencies. Your local county agent and your local FHA field office can fill you in.

Investigate FHA and VA mortgage loan insurance. Mortgage loan insurance provided by these agencies will often provide the kicker you need to sell one of your properties. Furthermore, if you have cash, you can retain it for business purposes (rather than housing) by living in a mortgaged house. Some entrepreneurs get started by selling the clear homes or large equities that they've accumulated. Then they put up a low down payment and take a big mortgage on another house. They put the freed cash to work in their business.

Contact FHA and VA for details on their programs. The FHA publishes:

Digest of Insurable Loans,
HUD PG-4 (20¢)

This publication gives essential background on Titles I, II, VII, VIII, and X. You'll be surprised at the scope of the various sections under these titles. For example, you'll discover that you can get FHA loan insurance for a multiple-unit income-producing property. You can get up to 90 percent financing too!

A large number of agencies make or guarantee loans. For example, Commodity Credit Corporation and Farmers Home Administration administer a multiplicity of programs that will prove valuable to you if you farm. Department of the Interior has programs to encourage domestic minerals exploration, to assist in strengthening the domestic fishing industry, and to assist in reclamation and land development.

The Export-Import Bank of the United States has programs to assist exporters. The Agency for International Development has programs to assist private developers in less developed countries and to assist American businessmen in foreign business development and expansion. The Department of Health, Education and Welfare guarantees loans for students pursuing college degree programs, including special programs for medicine, dentistry, osteopathy, and optometry.

> *Moonlight Fortune Tip (MFT) 6*
> Investigate the government loan and loan
> guarantee possibilities for financing your
> moonlight ventures.

RECIPROCAL DEALS PAY OFF

Small businessmen scratch each other's backs. This is the most elementary form of reciprocity. Merchant A buys all of his insurance from Insurance Agent B. Insurance Agent B buys all of his groceries from Merchant A. Insurance Agent B buys his office supplies from Manufacturer C. Manufacturer C buys his insurance from Insurance Agent B. This kind of reciprocity has existed since the earliest days of history. Frequently businessmen make specific reciprocal deals. The reciprocity forms a kicker for each man in the deal. Keep this Moonlight Fortune Tip in mind.

> *Moonlight Fortune Tip (MFT) 7*
> Utilize kickers—reciprocity, interlocking
> deals, discounts, bonuses, and sweeteners—
> to make big deals materialize.

HOW TO MAKE KICKERS INCREASE SALES

One of the most powerful applications of the kicker is in making a sale. These ingredients are essential before you can make a sale:

1. A person who has a need for the product or service that you are trying to sell;

2. That person must have the capability to pay for the product or service;

3. He must be authorized to buy and pay for it.

A deal frequently tends to fall down (especially when large amounts of money are involved) when you get to the matter of money. There are many mechanisms available to help you at this point, and the greatest of all is credit. If you're trying to sell a $10,000 house and your very warm prospect has only a few hundred dollars, it may seem impossible to sell it to him. But there is a way to consummate the deal if you're willing to exercise a little resourcefulness and do a little work. FHA, VA, and conventional loans are available. So are bank loans.

Suppose that your buyer cannot fully satisfy the requirements for minimum cash down payment. Suppose he needs $800 cash to buy the house. He has only $200. How can you sell it to him? Here's one approach. Put the house on contract of sale, get his $200, and then he pays you an amount each month till his total payments have reached $800 plus interest. At that point, you take the contract of sale, get his FHA, VA, or conventional loan, and close the deal.

Suppose you are selling equipment to a school. The school cannot afford the equipment. If you'll take a look into the various Titles that are available through the Department of Health, Education and Welfare, you can possibly find a Title under which part or perhaps all of the price of the equipment can be bought by the school with government help.

Discounts are another form of the kicker. Book publishers sometimes offer books at discounted prices prior to publication in order to have a large number of orders on hand when the book emerges from the bindery. You can use the same idea in launching a new product. The 2 percent discount for cash on sales by wholesalers has, over the years, helped most wholesalers secure prompt payment. You can use the same idea in your own business. Another application of the discount is for larger orders, hence 10 percent discount for quantities of 10 or more, 15 percent discount for quantities of 50 or more. The discount is a useful and profitable kicker.

The "premium" or "free with your order" sweetener is another form of kicker. So is the guarantee. The power of these kickers is evidenced by their frequent use in mail order advertising. Trading stamps are effective kickers in retail operations.

An extra service, such as free delivery, 30-day charge accounts, free monogramming, or free gift wrapping, is another form of kicker. If you maintain a service shop in conjunction with a product sales operation, the customer tends to write the availability of service in his mind as a kicker.

HOW TO USE KICKERS TO OBTAIN LOANS

I've already told you about how a friend of mine used the need to purchase an insurance policy to fulfill his need to finance a property. The kicker is used extensively both in getting and in dispensing loans. It is a common practice to discount loans on properties so that the lender gets an additional amount of money over and above the interest that accrues from the loan. When the FHA interest rates are below the prevailing commercial interest rates, the lender usually demands that the seller of the property pay "points."

Your banker always demands a kicker when he makes a loan. The kicker may be in the form of collateral. If the loan is made on your signature, you can bet your life that he's betting on your potential and looking into the future when you will be a bigger customer and a bigger borrower.

INTERLOCKING DEALS HELP EVERYBODY

Frequently situations arise where the required resources for setting up a business are greater than those that you have available. Sometimes you can find others who have interests in similar ventures or in related ventures which, when working together can get everybody what he wants, or nearly what he wants.

One of my friends got interested in a delivery service. However, in order to operate the delivery service, he needed a place where he could keep the trucks, a place where the calls could be made, and service for his vehicles. He made a deal with a service station operator to use his service station as headquarters. The service station operator provided the facility without any rental charge and agreed to take calls that related to the delivery business of my friend. In return, he got my friend's gas and servicing business which was quite sizable. Consequently, both my friend and the service station operator made out on the deal.

Another friend obtained a street cleaner which he used to sweep shopping center parking lots. He made a similar arrangement for storing his street sweeper and the trailer that he carried it on at a service station. In return for this storage space, he gave the service station operator all of his gas and service business.

It sometimes seems that one of the biggest problems of the fortune builder is his borrowing power. Credit is a very valuable tool and no real fortune builder can ever seem to get enough of it. One of my friends had a number of properties and had used his credit up to the hilt. The properties were throwing off good cash, but he was only able to service his existing debt. He wasn't able to expand. The insurance business that was involved with his properties amounted to $5,000 a year. One of the insurance agencies in town also did some mortgage lending. My friend approached the owner of the agency with this proposition: If you'll obtain a $10,000 mortgage for me on a piece of property that I want to buy, I'll throw the insurance business on all of my property over to you in the future. The agency owner agreed and my friend added another property to his stable. This added approximately $1,000 a year to his spendable cash. The insurance agency owner was so happy with the business that he later helped him get additional mortgage loans which added further to my friend's spendable cash flow.

Here's another case of an interlocking deal. Mr. A. is a writer and he wanted to publish one of his own books. He had limited funds, so he approached B., a printer, with this proposition: "If you'll print my books on credit and allow me to pay you as I sell them, I'll give you an additional royalty of 5 percent on every book that is sold." Thus by allowing the printer to make a multiple profit, Mr. A. was able to publish his own book and consequently reap a higher profit.

Or take the case where you are starting a new business. You need $10,000 in order to finance the business. You approach an investor to borrow $10,000. He does not see any particular merit in lending you $10,000 because he sees that there is some risk involved in your business. But let's assume that in your business you will be selling furniture. The investor that you approach builds houses. You make a deal with him to lend furniture to him for use in his sample houses and agree to sell furniture to him at a discount when he needs it. Everybody makes out on this interlocking deal.

Interlocking deals that involve big money are frequently made in real estate. The aggressive real estate agent has several sellers. Seller A might take the kind of property that B has in trade. But B doesn't want A's property. The real estate agent finds a seller C who has the kind of property B will take and who is willing to take A's property in trade. Hence, the agent earns three commissions by making a three-way interlocking trade. The traders gain tax advantages in the process.

MULTIPLE PROFITS SWEETEN DEALS

You can make multiple profits in your business. Multiple profits are most common in real estate investment and associated businesses. Realtors, for example, are always anxious to work trades. Why? Because they get multiple profits. They get a commission from each of the traders and consequently the commission may be double, triple, or even four times the commission that they would earn by selling the originally listed property for cash. Another way that multiple profits are earned in real estate transactions is through the use of the first lien and second lien notes by the seller where the seller in essence finances the property he sells. So he makes a capital gains profit from the sale of the property and an ordinary income gain in the form of interest on the loan.

If you rent a property, that is, if you have real estate and rent it to a tenant unfurnished, your cash pull is smaller than if you rent the property furnished. In addition to securing a profit through the rental of the real property, you obtain a profit through the rental of the furniture. You can carry this a step further and furnish utilities at a profit. This is why many investors who seek to pyramid their fortunes rapidly invest in apartment houses and furnish utilities and furniture.

Now, let's leave real estate deals and talk about double profits in other businesses. Assume you are a distributor of school supplies. You call on drug stores and supermarkets that carry school supplies and do a very heavy business during the months of August and September, and then on a continuing but lower volume basis through the school months. You're buying all of your school supplies from the manufacturer. You can make multiple profits by becoming a manufacturer yourself (and incidentally, most large school supply distributors are also manufacturers) and printing your own graph paper and your own tablets. You might resort to packaging your own papers; e.g., buying notebook paper in bulk and packaging it yourself. You might double profit by coming up with some special notebook subject separators that have calendars, conversion tables, or blank schedule forms printed on them. You might start publishing and printing (on contract with a printer) books to help students study better.

Perhaps you have a store which sells electric lighting fixtures.

You can double profit by manufacturing light fixtures in your back room, perhaps some antique lamps or reproductions of antique-type lamps, or some zany novelty lamps—things of this sort.

Or suppose that you're in the automobile leasing business. Most automobile leasing companies, such as Hertz, Avis, and National, wholesale their cars after they replace them. If you're a small operator with a small automobile leasing operation, you can reap additional profits by retailing your used cars yourself.

MORE MULTIPLE PROFIT GIMMICKS

If you're a manufacturer of a product, you can multiply profits on the product by making minor variations in the basic product so that the product serves additional markets. Radio and television set manufacturers profit in this manner by using the same chassis in several different models or types of cabinets.

If you sell furniture you can double profit by manufacturing some special types of furniture in your back room. For example, you might obtain unfinished Early American furniture and simply finish it and then offer it for sale finished. One of my friends, Mr. Mayten of Dallas, has built a business on selling unfinished furniture and furniture that he finishes himself.

Night clubs and entertainment spots long ago learned and employed the principle of multiple profits. The movie theater makes multiple profits by selling programs, soft drinks, popcorn, candy, and other refreshments. They make it a point to put a plug for the refreshment stand on the screen just prior to the intermission. Popcorn sells drinks, and hence multiplies profits. Night clubs did it long ago with the cover charge and with the minimum. Airports would be totally unprofitable without the income from the various concessions, which include the shops in the terminal building, the car rental agencies, the parking lots, and numerous others.

Another way to make a multiple profit is to sell an item and repurchase it later at a lower price. Helena Rubenstein sold her cosmetic business for $7.5 million and one year later repurchased it for $1 million. In some cases, financial failure on the part of the buyer makes an exceptional repurchase available to you. In other cases, loss of interest by the purchaser or lack of utility to the purchaser makes it possible for you to repurchase a product at a very advantageous price.

There are a number of double profit gimmicks that apply to the utilization of your money. For example, you can purchase stock with your cash, take the stock down to the bank and borrow approximately 50 percent of the market value in most banks in the United States. You must use the proceeds of the loan for other uses than the purchase of *listed* securities.

Another means of making a multiple profit is to own the building in which you have your business. If you own the building, you make the profit that would ordinarily go to another owner. Consequently, after a period of 10 or 20 years, your building is paid off and has value. If you rent the building, you have nothing at the end of this period of time. There are some extenuating factors in connection with cash requirements and the present tax laws which might make it wiser to rent than to purchase.

Manufacturers multiply profits horizontally and vertically. A manufacturer applies vertical profit multiplication by increasing his span from raw material to end product; i.e., by manufacturing his own subassemblies, components, and even processing his own raw materials. He can carry the process further in his marketing by becoming his own wholesaler, even to the point of owning or participating in his retail outlets.

A manufacturer can multiply his profits through horizontal expansion into related products and businesses that utilize his existing facilities, marketing organization or some other facet of his existing business.

MAKE THE KNOWLEDGE KICKER WORK FOR YOU

You obviously have a better chance of success in your business if you know quite a bit about it. Because you know some business or discipline well doesn't mean that you have to restrict your activities to that endeavor. You can always learn a new business or a new discipline. But be sure that you do learn it—either by working in it, or through study, observation, discussion, and practice. Luther H. has a camera store. He outsells every other camera dealer in town because he knows cameras backwards and forwards. He gives his customers full verbal instructions on how to use the cameras they purchase, and he's always willing and ready to give them advice over the phone on picture-taking. His know-how gives his business an extra dimension—an extra kicker—for his customers.

> *Moonlight Fortune Tip (MFT) 8*
> Use the knowledge kicker. Know your business and share your knowledge with your customers.

THE TIMING KICKERS MAKE AMAZING PROFITS

Retailers time their product promotions to events and seasons. They promote Christmas gift items before Christmas, and they take advantage of Mother's Day, Father's Day, Thanksgiving graduation time, and other seasonal events. They promote summer, outdoor and lawn equipment in late winter and spring. They promote winter clothes and equipment in the late summer and fall. They time their promotions to prescheduled holidays and to the season cycle.

The customer who wants something now, provides an opportunity to capitalize on the timing kicker. If you can deliver immediately and your competitor cannot, you'll make the sale.

Quick footwork is part of the strategy in capitalizing on the timing kicker. For example, the launching of Sputnik stimulated manufacturers of scientific toys to capitalize on the event by stepping up the production of new educational and scientific toys. They related their promotions to Sputnik and the need for scientific education in the U.S.A. More frequent examples of fast footwork have been presented by the publishing industry which has been quick to introduce titles relating to the cigarette-cancer scare, the Warren Commission Report, and the report on the Chicago riots.

Moonlight Fortune Tip (MFT) 9
Make the timing kicker work for you by tapping seasonal and cyclical demands and by reacting quickly to random events.

THE WEALTH-BUILDING KICKER CHECKLIST

A. Money and Material Kickers
1. Cash with Order
2. Discounts
3. Easy Financing
4. Government Loans and Subsidies
5. Premiums
6. Trading Stamps
7. Contests and Door Prizes
8. Business Reciprocity
9. Horizontal and Vertical Profit Multiplication
10. Low Prices

B. Service Kickers
1. Delivery
2. Telephone Order Taking
3. Fast Service
4. Installation
5. Guarantees

6. Information Pamphlets
7. Verbal Instructions and Counsel
8. Ship Anywhere
9. Charge Accounts
10. Gift Wrapping

4

SCIENTIFIC PRINCIPLES FOR NO-RISK FORTUNE BUILDING

SCIENCE AND METHOD MAKE BIG MONEY

Fortunes can be built without scientific methods. But if scientific methods are applied in your wealth-building program, the going is easier and faster. The techniques, strategies, and plans that we will discuss in this chapter are based on the application of proven business principles as well as new ways of looking at things. You may find this chapter particularly exciting because you'll suddenly discover that you're thinking about business and moneymaking in a totally different and more productive way. There's something else, too.

You can accumulate a fortune without really knowing too much about "how to speak the language." But being able to speak the language makes the quest for a fortune easier. When you are able to speak the language, it's like putting oil on a squeaking wheel—the wheel runs more smoothly, faster, and longer. Being able to speak the language will do the same thing for you when you go to the bank to discuss loans, when you're negotiating deals, and when you're preparing ads and publicity

73

to build your business. Here's an example of how this worked for Jim W.

Jim W. had been trying to build a moonlight income in property investments for a number of years. He bought properties and tried to operate them as successful rentals. He couldn't get a good yield on his first property, so he sold it with a very small down payment. His buyer defaulted and by the time Jim got the property back, he had lost quite a bit of money. He tried renting again. But his renters damaged the property and a series of poor paying tenants stuck him for rent time and again. His resources were stretched to the hilt and he had to sell the property. I bought it from him, and in a matter of three months, I had turned it into an extremely lucrative rental property.

A few months later, Jim had accumulated some new funds. He hit on a new plan for getting back into property investment and he told me about it. His plan seemed ill conceived and I suggested he take time to learn some of the scientific principles of moonlight fortune building. He was reluctant to take the time and spend the money for the program I proposed, but he finally decided to pursue it. That was just four months ago. Today he has two profitable rental properties and he's enlarging his capability for more profitable investment by continuing his study and consultation program. If he continues at his present rate of progress, he'll control a million-dollar business empire in five to ten years.

> *Moonlight Fortune Tip (MFT) 10*
> Learn and apply the ten scientific principles for no-risk fortune building.

THE TEN AMAZING NO-RISK FORTUNE BUILDING PRINCIPLES

One or more of the no-risk fortune building principles that will be discussed in this chapter were used in amassing every fortune of substance throughout reported history. They form a basic philosophy applicable to any and all business ventures. In treating these principles in this chapter, I've endeavored to apply science and technology to the discussion. This approach extends their scope and stand, and will help to burn them in your mind. Here they are.

1. The No-Risk Family Security Principle
2. The Percentage of Cash-in-Return Investment Principle
3. The Principle of Spendable Cash Flow Evaluation and Optimization
4. The Powerful Principle of Fast Growth Turnover
5. The Perpetual Income Principle of Continuing Return
6. The Pyramiding Principle of Compounded Turnover and Integrated Income
7. The No-Investment–High-Return Principle of Intangibles
8. The Sure-Income Hedging Principle of Diversification
9. The Powerful Principle of Synergistic Expansion
10. The Principle of Working Resource Optimization

THE NO-RISK FAMILY SECURITY PRINCIPLES

The no-risk family security principle is the basis of this book. It's simply this: Maintain a sure family support income while you venture into fortune and estate-building businesses and investments. Initially this means that most of us must maintain full-time employment that provides the resources that we need to support our family. Your fortune building ventures should in no way interfere with the optimum performance of your job at your place of employment. Give your employer everything and more than he deserves in return for the salary that he pays you. Perform your job so well that you place yourself in line for a continuing series of raises. Every time that your salary increases, your venture capability increases, too. Utilize your savings, a regular portion of your income, and all the credit that you can secure to engage in your fortune building ventures.

The No-Risk moonlight approach to fortune building is not as fast as a full-time, undiluted, single-minded approach. But, the moonlight approach reduces the possibility of failure to near zero. Furthermore, the moonlight approach avoids the delay that is frequently introduced in the accumulation of a nest egg for a full-time pursuit.

THE MONEY-MAKER'S WAY OF DETERMINING RETURN ON INVESTMENT

The business venturer may use any of a large number of criteria for determining the success of his ventures. Most successful investors determine their success by measuring the return on investment. Other useful ratios to the businessman and to the investor are based on sales, profits, turnover, or any other of a host of criteria. Here are just a few of the methods that are used by successful investors:

1. Percentage return based on total cost of investment.

2. Percentage return based on total cost of investment and total expense.

3. Percentage return based on actual cash spendable against initial cash investment.

4. Percentage of net profit return on gross sales.

For purposes of discussion, the following figures pertain to a property that was acquired for investment purposes:

Property	$100,000
Down Payment	10,000
Annual Payment	15,000 Plus Interest at 6%
Maintenance and Operating Cost	5,000
Allowable Annual Depreciation	4,000
Annual Gross Income	30,000

If you apply criteria 1 above to this investment, you have a gross income of $30,000 against a property cost of $100,000, or a return of 30 percent. If you apply criteria number 2, you have the annual gross income of $30,000 minus the maintenance cost of $5,000, minus the first year interest cost of $5,400; hence, the net income is $19,600. This produces a return of 19.6 percent of the total investment. If you apply criteria number 3, you use the annual gross income of $30,000 minus maintenance and operating costs of $5,000, the annual payment of $15,000, and the $5,400 interest for the first year, you have net spendable cash of $4,600. $4,600 divided by the down payment of $10,000 (the actual cash invested) gives you a return of 46 percent. This is very meaningful. Note, too, that most of this $4,600 return is sheltered completely by the allowable annual depreciation of $4,000. (I've cited the allowable annual depreciation for tax purposes only. It is assumed that the depreciation is covered by the maintenance and operating costs.)

Criteria number 4 is based on the net profit return on gross sales. It doesn't have anything to do, directly that is, with the amount of the investment. In this case, to have a basis for taking the property value into account, we'll use the allowable annual depreciation as a cost basis for the property. Then the profit is the annual gross income minus the maintenance and operating costs, minus the first year's interest, minus the allowable depreciation. The resulting profit is $15,600. If you divide this by the total annual gross sales of $30,000, the result is a 52 percent net profit on sales.

The money-maker uses these and variations of these methods for determining return on investment. The most meaningful method for the resource-limited investor to use is method number 3—Percentage return based on actual cash spendable against initial cash investment. This method is the most meaningful and the most powerful criterion to apply to the evaluation of any investment because it shows the percentage return on dollars invested now; and dollars to invest now are usually the scarcest resource of the beginning investor. For example, a down payment of $20,000 on this property would hardly influence any of the other parameters. The interest payment would be reduced slightly and this would reflect a minor change in other parameters. Consequently there'd be minor changes in the percentage return reflected by most of the criteria. However, method number 3—Percentage return based on actual cash spendable against initial cash investment—would reflect a significant change. Actual cash spendable would increase from $4,600 to $5,200. But this would be compared against an initial cash investment which has increased from $10,000 to $20,000. Consequently, instead of a 46 percent return, the return is reduced to 26 percent.

It is significant to note that criteria number 3 will be enlarged directly in proportion to the enlargement of the numerator and inversely in proportion to the enlargement of the denominator. Consequently, anything that you can do to increase the annual gross income and reduce the annual payment, the annual interest, and the annual maintenance and operating costs will increase the percentage return. And anything that you can do to decrease the amount of the down payment or actual cash investment will also contribute to increasing this percentage.

The money-maker's primary criterion for determining return on investment is based on the actual cash spendable against the initial cash investment. All other criteria are secondary except in special, specific situations.

THE PRINCIPLE OF SPENDABLE CASH FLOW OPTIMIZATION

The preceding principle is the key to the principles of spendable cash flow optimization. Spendable cash income determines the capability of the investor and businessman to increase the size of his total investment in both cash and borrowed form.

Consequently, anything that you can do to increase the spendable cash income from your business and consequently the cash flow of your business accelerates growth in multiple, compounding, integrating form through the application of the ten fortune building principles presented here.

These ten practices will optimize spendable cash flow:

1. Increase prices
2. Increase gross sales volume
3. Minimize cash investment
4. Maximize borrowing
5. Seek longest loan terms
6. Seek lowest loan interest rates
7. Charge purchases and take maximum allowed payment time without forfeiting discounts and without accruing penalties
8. Always take discounts
9. Cut operating expenses
10. Convert unavoidable variable costs into fixed percentage costs wherever possible.

Exercise practical judgment in implementing these practices in your business and in employing the no-risk fortune building principles presented in this chapter. You can overdo these principles to the point where your financial situation becomes precarious and unstable. Always make good judgment prevail.

THE POWERFUL PRINCIPLE OF FAST GROWTH TURNOVER

If you have $10,000 with which to buy goods that you can resell for $20,000, you'll realize a gross profit of $10,000. If you can do this only once in the course of a year, your annual profit is $10,000 gross. However, if you can invest your $10,000 twice during the course of a year, you can realize a $20,000 gross profit. If you can increase even further the number of times that you can turn your money over, your linear gross profit will increase by the number of times that you create a turnover.

Now suppose that you can turn over two times a year any amount you invest. Hence, if you start with $10,000, after your first turn you'll have $20,000; then, if you invest this $20,000, after the next turn you'll have $40,000. Consequently, with only two turnovers of your available resources, you have made the equivalent profit of three linear turnovers. The factors that are used in determining turnover and the meaning of the resulting ratios varies widely in the business world. We won't embroil ourselves in discussion of the subject here. The big point in the powerful principle of fast growth turnover is to make your available money work as hard as possible during any given unit of time.

THE PERPETUAL INCOME PRINCIPLE OF CONTINUING RETURN

When a merchant invests $10,000 in inventory for his store, he can realize a one-time return from the sale of that inventory. If he doesn't reinvest the money which he realizes from the sale, the sale produces no further income. This is a one-time return.

When a lender lends $10,000 for a term of ten years at 8 percent, he has a continuing return for a period of ten years. He receives a return of $800 per year. The continuing fixed return results from loan investments, bond investments, and some property rent-lease investments.

If you make a $10,000 investment in an equity, you have a perpetual income possibility as well as a perpetual growth possibility. Hence, if you take an equity position in a company through the purchase of stock or through a partnership, your income continues to grow as the business grows, and you have an income as long as the business continues to exist. Theoretically, a business can continue forever. Hence, an equity investment can produce perpetual income. Property investments generally produce perpetual income and possess the possibility of perpetual growth. Continuing return is reasonably sure for the life of the building and other improvements on the property. By the time the building becomes unproductive or physically unsound, urban growth usually forces land appreciation to values that provide substantial continuing returns. Since chain of title is continuous, a property investment has the possibility of producing perpetual income.

To capitalize on the perpetual income principle of continuing returns, seek investments which involve equity positions in businesses and properties. These investments will generally provide continuing returns, continuing income growth, and they will require a minimum of future bother and effort.

THE PYRAMIDING PRINCIPLE OF COMPOUNDED TURNOVER AND INTEGRATED INCOME

The pyramiding principle of compounded turnover and integrated income was introduced during the discussion of principle number 4—the powerful principle of fast growth turnover. Capitalize on compounded turnover growth by reinvesting the profits of your business along with the returned principal as fully and as rapidly as possible. Hence, you compound your turnover and a few turns provide substantially increased annual profits. Compounded turnover has an integrating effect on net worth. If in your mathematical studies you had the opportunity to learn calculus, you may recall that the accumulated effects of change on initial values are found by the process of integration. Integration of income into net worth (principal) accelerates the growth of net worth.

THE NO-INVESTMENT–HIGH-RETURN PRINCIPLE OF INTANGIBLES

If you apply the recommended criteria of principle number 2 to an investment of $0 which provides a finite income, the percentage of return gropes to reach infinity. Consequently, if you don't have to invest any money and can still earn a return, you can do quite well as a businessman.

We pointed out earlier that there are ventures which do not require any cash investment. These ventures generally involve the exploitation of an intangible. They're based on the exploitation of an idea or of "sweat" equity in the form of mental or physical work. The investor with limited dollar resources should concentrate his attention on the exploitation of intangibles. Hence, while he may be limited on his cash investment ventures, he can exploit intangibles for infinite-yield profit possibilities.

Typical no-investment–high-return exploitation of intangibles includes inventing, consulting, specialized services, commission salesmanship, writing, painting (art), and performing (entertainers).

THE SURE-INCOME HEDGING PRINCIPLE OF DIVERSIFICATION

Hedging is the process of minimizing an investment risk by taking an offsetting position. One way to take an offsetting position is to make an investment sufficiently unrelated to the basic investment that factors (social, economic, legislative, regulatory, etc.) disturbing to one investment will not affect the other. This process is *diversification*. Defense contractors diversify within their fields of endeavor by pursuing programs related to hot wars (so-called "brush wars"), as well as cold wars. Many defense contractors have diversified into commercial business so that their dependence on government contracts is minimized. The principle of diversification has led many companies into business fields that are totally new. This has resulted in the development of the so-called "conglomerate" corporation. You, as a million-dollar moonlighter can take the sure-income hedging route to profit through diversification even more readily than large corporations.

If you invest in residential income-producing properties, you can diversify your property holdings by adding commercial and industrial properties to your stable. If you're a building contractor, you can diversify by adding repair and modification services to your line of business. Hence, when new construction activity is down, you can capitalize on increased activity in repairs and remodeling. If you operate a restaurant, you can diversify by getting into food packing and by investing in businesses that produce foodstuffs for home consumption. Consequently, you can capitalize on changes in eating habits. The same approach applies in reverse to the food packer and the bakery operator. They can diversify through the operation of restaurants and food stands. If you sell appliances, you can diversify by adding appliance service to your business.

Your diversification does not have to be so nearly related to your basic business as the examples that I've just cited. Hence, if you're in the publishing business, you can diversify by making real estate investments, by acquiring equity positions in other manufacturing businesses, or by acquiring retailing interests as diverse as a chain of ladies' dress shops. The basic criterion for wise diversification that I wish to emphasize in this section and under this principle is that factors disturbing to one investment should not disturb your other investments. The next principle provides an additional guideline for diversification.

THE POWERFUL PRINCIPLE OF SYNERGISTIC EXPANSION

Synergistics is the process of combining two or more entities in such a way that the result is greater than the sum of the results obtainable separately. For example, a manufacturer of pen and pencil sets merges with a manufacturer of men's jewelry. As a result of the merger, the customer list for both products is increased. Some of the manufacturing facilities may be eliminated and the number of people serving in staff functions can be reduced. Consequently, sales for the two product lines should be greater than the sum of the pre-merger sales. Costs should be reduced below the sum of the operating costs of each of the individual entities. Hence, profits for the combined operation should increase substantially above the sum of the profits for the two individual operations.

The principle of synergistics can be applied in an infinite variety of ways. The most frequent way in which synergistics is applied to big business is through merger and diversification. You, as a million-dollar moonlighter, can make synergistics work for you in the same manner. Hence, although your first consideration in taking diversification action may be to provide a hedging situation, you can still take factors with synergistic effects into account. Consequently your diversification action can provide a hedge as well as a vehicle to synergistic growth.

Diversification is not the only path through which you can exploit synergistics. You can exploit synergistics in making individual deals, in mechanizing your business operation, and in financing your enterprises. Although you have to gear your thinking to the individual entities of your business ventures in the process of operation, you can experience greater growth and expansion if you'll gear your policy and growth thinking to your overall venture operations.

THE PRINCIPLE OF WORKING RESOURCE OPTIMIZATION

The principle resources of the million-dollar moonlighter are time, knowledge, skills, facilities, equipment, assistants, labor, and money. To build your wealth fast, you'll have to optimize your utilization of these resources. Avoid diversions, nit-picking, and underemployment of your talent that makes encroachments upon your time. Expand your knowledge and bring it to bear on the problems of your business. Utilize your skills to the hilt by proper utilization of assistants and labor. Make your facilities and equipment pay off by keeping them productive whenever possible. (I've always been amazed at the poor time utilization of school buildings and church buildings.) Compensate your assistants and your laborers in proportion to their direct contribution to product and profit. Make your cash money pull heavy loads by exploiting leverage and by keeping it invested.

Chapter 7 will deal further with utilizing your resources in optimum fashion, but proper utilization of resources in business and investment ventures is so important that I recommend considerable additional study on these subjects.

THE SCIENTIFIC WEALTH-BUILDING CHECKLIST

1. Minimize risk by keeping your full-time job while you build your moonlight fortune.

2. Evaluate business deals on the percentage return based on actual cash spendable against initial cash investment.

3. Optimize spendable cash flow by implementing the practices listed on page 78.

4. Accelerate growth by speeding turnover.

5. Build perpetual incomes by making investments with continuing returns.

6. Create substantial net worth rapidly by compounding turnover and integrating income.

7. Realize infinite returns on investment by exploiting "no cash required" intangibles.

8. Hedge your income against disturbances by diversifying your ventures.

9. Realize bigger profits and faster growth by applying the principles of synergistics.

10. Make your resources more productive by utilizing them wisely, continually, and aggressively.

5

TAP THE EIGHT PRINCIPAL WAYS IN WHICH ALL FORTUNES HAVE BEEN AND WILL BE MADE

ALL FORTUNE BUILDING APPROACHES ARE DOMINATED BY ONE OR MORE OF THESE EIGHT METHODS

There are eight principal ways in which all great fortunes were and will be made. These eight ways include just about any kind of business or investment that you can think of. As you survey these eight ways, you'll note that several of them are interrelated. Any specific business might use several of these in developing its profits. Here they are:

(1) Make a profit on natural resources.

(2) Make a profit through invention, creation, or the harnessing of a new technology.

(3) Make a profit in manufacturing or construction.

(4) Service your way to riches.

(5) Make a profit by selling products.

(6) Make a profit by leasing or renting real estate, services, and products.

(7) Make a profit by trading products, real estate, services, and negotiable instruments.

(8) Provide financing for others for business ventures, business growth, and/or the satisfaction of personal wants and needs.

Now, let's examine each of these eight fortune building approaches.

EXPLOIT NATURAL RESOURCES

Some of the greatest fortunes ever made have been in natural resources. Natural resources include the land (and therefore real estate), everything that is under the land (minerals, energy in the form of coal and oil, vegetation that grows in the ground and others), the vegetation that grows on the earth (including plants, food, flowers), the living creatures on the earth (livestock, pets, wild animals, rodents), the water (the seas, the lakes, rivers, brooks, ponds, pools), the living creatures in the water (fish, crustaceans, etc.), the minerals in the seas and in the water, the air around us, the sky above us, and the many delightful combinations that result from several of these, such as the seashore, the country resort, and the wooded lake.

The easiest way for the moonlight fortune builder to get into natural resource investments is through the purchase of common stocks. The more venturesome investor can speculate in natural resources through syndicates. Here's how an oil syndicate works. A promoter (generally a geologist in the business of development and exploration) determines that an area has an opportunity for producing oil or other output. The promoter secures mineral leases or options to purchase the land. He determines total cost of the leases for land acquisition and the exploration and drilling costs. He divides this total cost into a number of working interests (64 working interests are common), and he sells these interests to those who wish to join in the syndicate. The promoter may reserve working interests for himself, and he may make lease reservations for himself. The cost of a working interest to an investor might range from $1,000 or $2,000 on up. For example, one proposal that went out for a 1/64th working interest required the investor to put up $1,200 for land acquisition and exploration fees at the outset, and an additional investment of $2,000 for turnkey drilling costs at a later date. The estimated net to the working interest if the exploration resulted in a discovery was almost $5,000,000. The potential profit to risk was 118 to 1.

Rock hobbyists make considerably smaller investments in equipment and profit handsomely from their ventures. They spend their weekends looking for rocks and minerals that they literally pick up and collect at no cost whatsoever. Some rock hounds trade their raw mineral finds. Most of them finish and polish the rock they find before trading or selling it. Still others convert the rocks into jewelry and art objects.

Some investors make their bundle in forest products. A typical moonlighter investment in this area is the investment made by Mark R. Mark bought a hundred acres of Ozark land at $50 an acre. His total cost was $5,000. He bought the property for 10 percent down or $500 cash. Working through the Department of Agriculture and the County Agent, he had the trees on the property marked for cutting and then had the loggers move in. He collected $1,000 from the cuttings which provided space for the remaining trees to grow better. He also planted several thousand seedlings at practically no cost and will be able to make selective cuttings from the property every five or ten years. The income from the cuttings will pay for the land and provide a small amount of spendable cash. Meanwhile, his property is appreciating in value and by the time he has made the payments, it will be worth about five times what he paid for it.

James Brown, Jr., of Sand Point, Idaho, built a profitable business by working cut-over land. In 1939, with $500 of borrowed money, he obtained equipment to recover sunken logs from a lake in northern Idaho. The forests had been cut over years ago and many deadheads had been left behind. In one year's time, he sold $76,000 worth of lumber that he cut from the sunken logs.

In recent years, the ocean has received a considerable amount of attention. The oceans provide business opportunities in petroleum and minerals, the purification of ocean water, transportation, chemicals from the sea, food from the sea, power generation, and marine salvage, to mention only a few.

Salvage and reclamation of used resources is an extremely profitable business. We mentioned marine salvage in connection with the ocean. Angelo Tersini of San Francisco, made a fortune in tin cans. Tersini got into the used tin can business in 1924. Pineapple was shipped from Hawaii in No. 10 cans (capacity about 3 quarts) to fruit salad packers. When the contents were removed, the cans were thrown away. Tersini collected the cans and sold them as scrap metal.

Lewis F. is a school teacher. He likes the out-of-doors, and five years ago he bought 20 acres of land with 600 feet of lake front. Over the years, he spent his summer vacations improving this property and turning it into a resort. He installed picnic tables, cleaned up the beach, sanded portions of the beach, and built a large dormitory-type lodge. He now specializes in catering weekend outings which he is free to handle and in renting campsites during the summer. He has already paid for his property and all of the improvements on it and has recently purchased adjoining land to expand his operations. Hence, beaches and view property have resort potential and ultimate high resale values. This is another way for the small investor to capitalize on natural resource investments.

In Chapter 7, you'll discover additional ways to invest in and profit on natural resources, and you'll discover that there are many resources available to you which aren't natural resources. Regardless of your choice of business or investment area, Chapter 7 will help you to discover resources in your own home, garage, attic, and other places where you'd least expect to find them. These resources will prove valuable to you in your moonlighting fortune building ventures.

MAKE A BUNDLE WITH INVENTIONS, CREATIVE IDEAS AND NEW TECHNOLOGIES

Some of the biggest fortunes of all have been made in new technologies and in the application of creative talents to every facet of our business world and our private lives. The attractive aspect of this route to fortune building is that you can frequently turn the trick without any cash whatsoever. You simply pull an idea or concept out of your mind and convert it into immediate cash—or into future cash in the form of royalties or participation in a business as part or whole owner.

You can profit on people's ideas, too. Besides marketing your own ideas, you can invest in the ideas of others. For example, Henry Ford's original investors put up $28,000 and got a $250 million return. Some investors participate in Broadway productions. If the play goes, they strike it rich. Recently, I saw an ad in the *Wall Street Journal* where a writer offered investment participation in his forthcoming book. Arthur J. Rock invested in Teledyne, an applied science company, by buying 45,000 shares at $6.50 a share. At the time this was written, the stock was selling around $100 a share.

Creation is the process of taking the things that you know and putting them together in a different way to come up with a new way to do something, a new product, or a way to use something that is already available in a new and different way.

Invention is one form of creation, but the inventor is not the only kind of creator who reaps fortunes through his creative efforts. The inventor applies his creative processes in the technological fields and comes up with a new development—generally a new product. You can sell your invention, manufacture it yourself, or license someone else to manufacture it.

Some creative people operate with words and ideas on the printed page. The creation of the writer may take the form of speeches, lectures, textbooks, courses, instructions for doing something, or on the less practical but very necessary side, humor. He may sell his output at a fixed price, on a royalty basis, or he may publish his own works and profit directly from sales.

Another type of creator is the composer, a writer who deals not in words but in notes. The playwright and the script writer deal with the media of the stage, film, and TV. They're all creators. The performing artist uses the creations of the writer, composer and choreographer in creating his form of art.

The innovator, sometimes a designer, might design a new kind of house (an architect); or a new kind of dress (a dress designer); or a new artistic layout. The artist creates a breathtaking picture, a work of beauty, a work of art, a practical illustration for an advertisement, or a practical illustration to be used in the process of teaching. The artist generally works for a fixed fee or does speculative work to be sold at the best price the market will pay.

You must use your creative ability in turning a profit in any kind of business endeavor. Hence creativity plays a role in any business venture.

In Chapter 10, you'll be introduced to the numerous ways in which you can tap the profits in technology and new ideas. A large portion of this chapter is addressed to how to get bigger and better ideas, and to patents, copyrights, and the nitty-gritty of license and royalty negotiations.

MANUFACTURE OR CONSTRUCT YOUR WAY TO BIG BUCKS

Manufacturing is the process of taking raw materials, components, assemblies and subassemblies, and creating a final assembly that performs a useful service. We've all heard stories about people who manufacture in their homes. They start in a garage workshop, a small backyard electronics laboratory, or perhaps in the kitchen. (Incidentally, don't forget that a cake is a manufactured product.) Some moonlight manufacturers operate basement print shops. The builder is a manufacturer, too. He has the advantage of not needing a factory since he does his work on the building site.

Elliot Handler started Mattel, Inc., tops in toys in the U.S., when he visualized some wood scraps from his moonlight picture-framing venture converted into doll house furniture. Charles Kaman started Kaman Aircraft Corp. in the basement of his mother's home with $4,000 capital. Jerrold Electronics Corp. was started with a $450 cash investment by the founder.

Large factories often subcontract with individuals who have small garage shops for the manufacture of special components and subassemblies. There are many types of manufacturing, and we might take time to note some of the variations. For example, a converter takes raw material and converts it into another material—raw material for another manufacturer. The second manufacturer may take this raw material and convert it into components—small parts such as screws, knobs, and the like. Components are then sold to a third manufacturer who assembles them into subassemblies. These subassemblies are fabricated for another manufacturer who puts them into an end assembly.

Perhaps you're not interested in making money in your back-yard factory but are more interested in building houses, office buildings, hotels, motels, or apartment houses. There's plenty of money to be made in the construction business. Of course, it's a little more than building. One of the easiest ways to get started, especially in periods of high employment, is to get a moonlight job with someone in the business. You get to learn a lot of the tricks of the trade this way. As you get the hang of what goes on in the construction business, you'll gradually build the ground-work that you need to get going on your own.

The construction of a building generally takes the form of a series of deals and subcontracts wherein the developer has a number of lots to start with. He may contract with the builder to construct homes on his lots, or he may sell lots to the builder and let the builder erect and sell the homes. If the builder does not have a customer for the house at the time that he begins to build it, it's known as a speculation, or a "spec" house. The builder is building on speculation and feels he's going to be able to sell it by the time he has it finished or shortly thereafter.

The builder obtains financing from the bank in the form of a building loan at the time he begins construction. This loan assures him of the capital that he requires to finish the construction of the house. This loan remains in effect until he can get a buyer to take the house and cover the sale with cash or cash and a mortgagor's loan commitment.

Many fortunes have been made in construction. New methods and technology are making the construction business more profitable all the time. The offsetting factor that tends to decrease the profits in construction—labor's becoming very expensive—will also open new horizons in construction technology development. If you can come up with practical mass-production techniques that will lower construction costs considerably, you'll make a big fortune. There are some problems along the way. More about that later.

There's money to be made in the so-called reconstruction of houses. One man that I know built a fortune by buying old run-down properties and fixing them up and reselling them. His general pattern was: Buy an old run-down house for $3,000 to $5,000, spend $1,000 to $3,000 fixing it up, make a profit of $2,000 to $7,000 in selling it.

I'd like to call your attention to a form of manufacturing that I believe will play an increasing role in the American economy. This is re-manufacturing as opposed to manufacturing. The United States is one of the most wasteful economies in the world.

Each year we throw away billions and billions of dollars worth of product that still has a use. Our big businesses encourage waste. For example, the paper industry would just as soon never have waste paper find its way back into the re-manufacture process. The waste process is encouraged with throw-away cans, throw-away packages, and things of that sort.

Yet many products that are ostensibly worn-out or damaged in some way have plenty of value left, and repairs and re-manufacture are economically sound. Many businesses thrive on re-manufacturing. This field is a lucrative one that is easy for the moonlight fortune builder to enter. Automobiles, automobile engines, starters, television sets, vacuum cleaners, hi-fi equipment, furniture, appliances, photographic equipment, etc., are just a few of the items on which successful re-manufacturing businesses can be built.

In Chapter 8, you'll pick up plenty of insider profit pointers on starting your own manufacturing, construction, or re-manufacturing business.

SERVICE YOUR WAY TO RICHES

We already have noted in Chapter 1 that the service industry and the demand for services is growing at a faster rate than production. We can look for this trend to continue throughout the next several decades. The principal reason for this unusual growth in the service industries is that automation is taking over in the production industries; consequently, production is increasing more rapidly than the requirement for manpower in the production industries. This increased production is demanding an increasing array of services. But the service industry is not undergoing rapid advances in automation. A television set still requires a painstakingly slow trouble-shooting procedure and single craftsman approach when it requires repairs.

Another reason for the rapid growth of the service industry is that the American public has come to demand more services and the average American would rather hire someone to do it than do it himself. This set of conditions makes it possible for anyone with a little "get up and go" to service his way to riches. Perhaps this is the path that you want to take to build your fortune.

Service businesses are ideally suited to moonlight fortune building. You can generally operate a servicing business from your home, and you can generally work your business in your spare time. The capital equipment requirements are generally low, too. If your hobby activity parallels the service activity that you intend to engage in, you'll generally have most of the equipment that is needed. If you're going to provide business services, it's probable that you already own most of the office equipment required to render these services. A personal automobile will generally satisfy the rolling stock requirements of a service business. Hence the low cost of entry into service business is appealing in itself.

The big secret to success in the service business is to provide satisfactory service at a reasonable price. Property and device maintenance servicemen are notorious for their lack of customer finesse and for rendering unsatisfactory service at much too high a price.

Moonlight Fortune Tip (MFT) 11
Customer satisfaction is the secret to repeat
business and continuing success.

This Moonlight Fortune Tip applies to any kind of business in which you might engage. It applies particularly to the service business.

SELL YOURSELF TO RICHES

One of the best ways to amass a fortune without investing a penny is as a salesman. There are thousands of companies in the United States that will provide you with a selling kit at no charge at all to go out and sell their product. They'll pay you generously high commissions. If you want to sell any specific product badly enough, you can find someone who is just as anxious to take you on as a commissioned salesman to sell that product.

Selling may take the form of door-to-door salesmanship, selling in a store, selling to your friends through personal contacts, selling to business, selling by mail, or any other of a variety of forms.

You might consider taking a selling job in a store during the busy pre-Christmas season. While a second job does not fulfill the required characteristics of a fortune building program, it can be useful in acquiring experience and training. Stores and companies who hire salesmen frequently train them. Although the training is usually provided in a crash program, you will get this training in addition to the actual experience of selling on the store floor.

After you have acquired some experience selling in a department store, move out on your own and sell something on commission.

> *Moonlight Fortune Tip (MFT) 12*
> Salesmanship is basic to any business success. Learn it well!

LEASE AND RENT FOR BIG CONTINUOUS PROFITS

Large fortunes have been made in leasing and rentals. The earliest leasing and rental fortunes have been made in real estate. Hertz expanded the idea and began leasing automobiles. Business machine and computer manufacturers moved into the rental and leasing field. Ryder moved into the big-business industrial leasing field and literally leases anything that a business may require. Today, anybody can rent almost anything that he wants in thousands of rent-all businesses that have been established across the length and breadth of the nation.

Here's how you make money in rentals and leasing. You purchase an object—in this case let's talk about a floor buffer which is used to wax and polish floors. Assume that the buffer costs $100. You buy the buffer on time for $15 down. The balance is financed. You rent the buffer to the public for $2.00 a day. Let's assume that you can rent the buffer ten days a month. That brings you $20 a month. Assuming that you financed the buffer for a period of eighteen months, your payments on the buffer are $5 a month, plus 1 percent of the unpaid balance. Hence, your first payment would be $5 plus $.85 (1 percent of the unpaid balance of $85). So, allowing for your payment to principal and your 1 percent of the unpaid balance, your first payment on the buffer amounts to $5.85. But you collected $20; hence, you have a cash flow or spendable cash of $20 minus $5.85, or $14.15. In addition, you have paid off $5 of the principal value of the buffer. Hence your actual profit is $19.15! You got more than your initial investment back in a month!

This simple example illustrates how a fortune can be made in the rental business. You use a very low investment and high leverage. You retain possession of the actual product or property, but you collect from others for allowing them to use it.

The business is not quite as simple as I've indicated. From time to time, the buffer will require service. This will make it impossible for you to rent the buffer for a short period and you'll experience repair overhead that will cut into your profit. Furthermore, the buffer will eventually wear out and have to be replaced. But it will probably not wear out before you have depreciated it and taken an additional income through the tax shelter created by the depreciation of the buffer.

Since a rental unit, whether it be real estate, a tool, or some other device, does not draw income when it is not being used for a fee, you've got to do a good selling job in order to keep your equipment and property rented as much as possible. Selling plays an important role in almost any of the seven big money-making business fields that I've outlined. It is especially important, though, in renting and leasing.

> *Moonlight Fortune Tip (MFT) 13*
> Rent-lease activities are top money makers because the investment requirements are low, the rented property provides its own loan collateral, the renters make the loan payments, and there are additional spendable profits.

You'll look into the million-dollar moonlighting possibilities in the rent-lease business in detail in Chapter 10. There you'll probe the cash-freeing and tax advantages that accrue to the lessee—aspects that further help the lease business to boom in a big way.

TRADE YOUR WAY TO RICHES

Another way to build your fortune is through trading. Buying and selling is a form of trading. Trading as we will discuss it in this section refers to barter. You take a resource that you have and you trade it for another resource plus some boot. Consequently you have a new resource to trade plus additional spendable cash. Many millionaires started their business careers by bartering. For example, O. L. Nelms, a Dallas millionaire, started trading pocket knives when he was a youngster. I did some trading while I was going to high school. In the real estate field, properties are constantly being traded. One of the advantages that accrues in trading is that the payment of taxes is deferred. Hence, trading is attractive to big income earners.

Trading for profit has some of the elements of selling, manufacturing, and providing services to build your fortune. These three elements all contribute to building a fortune through trading. You may also find that you get into our next area of concern—that of finance—because frequently you have to extend credit. In effect you make a loan with the item that you trade as collateral in order to make a trade come off. Since you have the other party's trade-in and some cash boot, you profit even if he defaults. In the real estate business, the second mortgage is frequently used as a mechanism for extending credit in a trade. Chattel mortgages are frequently used for trades involving furniture and other durable goods.

One of the biggest trading businesses in the United States is the automobile business. Whenever a person acquires a new car or a better used car, he generally trades in his older car. There's always someone a little lower on the economic ladder ready and willing to buy the car that is being traded in.

One of the beauties of trading is that your inventory is self-replenishing. Each time you make a trade, you have at least as many merchandisable items as you started with. Consequently, you eliminate the time losses involved in ordering and shipping that are associated with straight selling. Your resources work harder and faster, and consequently you can have bigger turnovers.

In his book, *How I Turned One Thousand Dollars into a Million in Real Estate in My Spare Time*,[1] William Nickerson shows how to start with $1,000, buy a property in the $10,000 range and then trade up successively to very valuable and high-priced properties. This book is good reading for any part-time money-maker, and it is a must if you ever intend to become involved in real estate. Although I prefer to keep properties that I acquire for rental and lease, many fortunes have been made in pyramid trading of properties. (I take the position that if a property was a good buy, then there is no reason to dispose of the good buy. I like to retain the property and continue to profit from its rental and use. I would rather keep what I get and put

---

[1] Published by Simon & Schuster, Inc., New York, 1959.

additional cash into buying additional properties. However, both techniques are employed successfully by various investors. It all depends on your preferences.)

> *Moonlight Fortune Tip (MFT) 14*
> Trade and make some boot profit on each deal. Finance part of the boot if you must to make a deal.

FINANCING PAYS SURE NO-RISK PROFITS

Many fortunes have been made in financing and banking, but these fortunes are not made through simple interest 6 percent loans. The fortunes that are made in financing are made through the use of "kickers" which were discussed in Chapter 3. Consequently, loans made for profit are usually higher interest loans which, when reduced to simple interest, in reality bear 12 percent or greater interest. In addition, "kickers" such as discounting the loan and service charges add to the income. Hence, the yield to the lender is relatively high.

Another gimmick that is frequently used in connection with financing is to sell a product at a higher price on time than it would be sold for cash. You'll find shops of the kind that sell at high prices with very low weekly payments in every city in the nation. They cater to low-income people and make a profit supplying credit that is usually hard for these people to obtain.

The simple interest loan is figured on the basis of the rate of interest applied over the period of time that the money is actually used.

Hence, if you borrowed $1,000 at 6 percent simple interest for a period of 10 months, the interest would be computed as follows:

$$\$1,000 \times .06 \times \frac{10}{12} = \$50$$

If you borrowed $1,000, to be paid back at the rate of $100 per month plus 6 percent simple interest, the first and second payments would be made as follows:

$$(1) \quad \$1,000 \times \frac{6\%}{12} = \$5. \text{ First payment is } \$105.$$

$$(2) \quad \$ \; 900 \times \frac{6\%}{12} = \$4.50. \text{ Second payment is } \$104.50.$$

You'd pay a total of $27.50 in interest.

On the other hand, assume that you borrowed $1,000 to be paid back at 6 percent interest on the original principal amount in ten monthly payments. The interest would be computed in this manner:

$$\$1,000 \times .06 \times \frac{10}{12} = \$50. \text{ Interest per payment} = \frac{\$50}{10} = \$5$$

It is obvious that interest computed in this manner is being charged at almost twice the rate of simple interest.

This is the method that is frequently applied to installment charge accounts. Assume that you owe $100. This is to be paid out at the rate of $10 per month plus 1 percent of the unpaid balance. When you make the first month's payment, you pay $10 plus 1 percent of $90. Hence, you pay $10.90. In reality you're paying 12 percent! Most stores now charge 1½ to 2 percent of the unpaid balance. Hence, they collect 18 to 24 percent simple interest.

Discounting works in this fashion: Suppose you borrow $10,-000 payable $1,000 a month plus 8 percent simple interest. However, the lender insists the note be discounted 3 percent in order for him to make the loan. Three percent of $10,000 is $300. So the lender actually gives you only $9,700. But he gets back $10,000 plus interest on this face amount.

From these simple examples, it is easy to see that plenty of money can be made by financing other people's needs and wants.

If you decide to use this as your principal means of fortune building, be sure to investigate the lending laws in your state. Loan practices have been abusive at times in the past, and most states have passed legislation to limit interest rates and loan conditions.

In Chapter 11, there'll be more information on debt financing from the viewpoint of you as a borrower as well as a lender. I prefer to borrow rather than to lend. The long-term trend of the economy is inflationary, and dollar devaluation is likely. Consequently, long-term loans are paid off with more easily gotten future dollars. The lender who gets his principal back in the future can buy less with it than it would buy today.

Moonlight Fortune Tip (MFT) 15
Be a borrower. Lend only when its essential in making a deal or a profit. Lend for the shortest term possible. Get a kicker for making the loan. Always insist on collateral.

6

THE SECRETS OF PROFITABLE TRADING

TRADING—PART OF ANY VENTURE

Trading is part of any business venture. You trade when you buy; you trade when you sell; you trade when you barter; you trade whenever you close any business deal. The emphasis on trading is greater in some businesses than in others. Hence, the stock market investor who works short-term gains, "trades." The commodity market investor is usually considered a trader. I like to think of anyone who engages in a good bit of barter as a trader.

THE 11 RULES OF PROFITABLE TRADING

The trader may do his trading in natural resources, ideas and inventions, manufacturing and re-manufacturing, services, products, leases, notes, commodities or stocks and bonds. If you weren't a trader at heart, you probably wouldn't be reading this book.

The trader is an innovator, a salesman, a negotiator, an appraiser, a manager, and an organizer. He has plenty of savvy concerning leases, rentals, and financing. Here are 11 rules that the astute trader follows in making his deals:

1. The trader looks for profit in a cash boot when he barters.

2. The trader builds and upgrades the value of what he "takes in" before he "trades it out."

3. The trader keeps what he makes on trades by avoiding bad trades from which he cannot profit and by making trades that provide advantageous tax positions.

4. The trader negotiates profitable trades.

5. The trader keeps trade deals open and avoids negotiation cutoffs.

6. The trader reaps big profits in apples and oranges (unlike) trades.

7. The trader knows how to find special situations.

8. The trader utilizes special information techniques.

9. The trader times for maximum profit trade.

10. The trader makes it easy to trade.

11. The trader profits on arbitrage.

The ensuing sections will explore these profitable trading rules and other aspects of trading your way to a fortune.

THE LOOT IS IN THE BOOT—PARTIALLY

There are two ways to trade. You can either trade up or you can trade down. The trader who is trading up provides a property or product of lesser value for a property or product of greater value. In trading up, he pays a cash boot and possibly assumes indebtedness to the other trader or another lender. For the trader who is trading up, the loot is in the boot in the sense that he can minimize the amount of cash that he pays and assume most of the difference in the form of a debt. The debt is a part of the boot although it isn't in the form of cash. Hence, resources can be increased with minimum cash outlay. In trading up, you'll want to be sure that the value of the equity that you are getting in the property for which you're trading up has greater potential than the cost basis of your property plus the boot.

On the other hand, if you're trading down, you always want to try to get as much boot as possible out of the trade. If you can take a portion of the boot in the form of a note secured by the traded item at a good rate of interest, that's fine and dandy. But be sure that the sum of the cash boot and the debt boot is adequate to yield a profit on the transaction.

HOW TO BUILD AND UPGRADE VALUES

The astute trader always builds the value of property that he takes in for trade before he puts up for trade. He may upgrade the value in the physical sense by improving or repairing it. In addition he builds the value by building intangible values into the product. The building of intangible value is a skill that stands any money-maker in good stead. Intangible value doesn't cost you a thing. All it takes is the innovative ability to discover and to communicate this intangible value to your potential buyer or trader.

Moonlight Fortune Tip (MFT) 16
In trading, look for upgrading potential in
anything you take in.

The trader can add value to a product simply by finding an anxious seller and anxious buyer. Hence, a man who has bought a new car and kept his old one to sell himself may suddenly become an overwilling seller. This happens when he can't sell the excess car over a period of time after several "asking price" reductions. The astute trader looks for a person who's anxious for this kind of car. When he finds an anxious buyer, he buys the car at a reduced price, sells at the higher price, and makes a nice profit for his effort.

Moonlight Fortune Tip (MFT) 17
The trader makes sure profits by finding
anxious buyers and anxious sellers.

HOW TO KEEP WHAT YOU MAKE IN TRADES

A trader cannot become emotional. Otherwise, he'll accumulate a lot of intangible values that he won't be able to dispose of profitably. Approach every trade deal realistically with a firm and logical appraiser's eye. In the event that you are trading in a property or a product where you have limited expertise, it is a good idea to obtain the services of an expert appraiser. In small deals, you may not feel that an appraisal fee is warranted; however, you can probably find someone in your sphere of associations who is not a professional appraiser, but who knows values in the specific area you are trading. Ask his advice. You "trade" favors with him by giving him similar assistance in your areas of knowledge when he needs it.

> *Moonlight Fortune Tip (MFT) 18*
> Buy on logic and realism—never on emotion.

If you buy or take a property in trade at a realistic price you can count on a profit when you retrade it. But, there are additional factors working for you that help you to keep the profits that you make in trade. These additional factors accrue to you as a result of the U.S. income tax laws.

First of all, even barter doesn't cost either party a cent at the time of the trade. Thus, a house and lot traded for another house and lot without any boot does not create an immediate tax liability for either party. The cost basis of the property received is the current value of the originally owned property. Thus, trader A has a property which cost him $10,000 ten years ago. He valued the lot at $1,000 and the house at $9,000. On a 30-year depreciation schedule, his current cost basis is $6,000 plus $1,000, or $7,000. Trader A makes an even property trade with trader B. The house that trader A receives is valued at $7,000 for tax purposes. He uses this value for subsequent depreciation and to arrive at his taxable gain when he sells the property.

Trader A's property may have appreciated to a value of $15,-000, and the property which he received from B may have a value of $12,000 on his books. Nevertheless, the new property will be carried on A's books at $7,000. If a year from now he sells it for $18,000, his profit for tax purposes is $18,000 minus $7,000, minus one year's depreciation. *Trader A pays no income tax on his trade now.* He can pyramid the value by making a series of trades. *He doesn't pay tax on even trades of like properties till he converts the property to cash or unlike property.* Hence, a trader keeps what he makes on trades till he converts it to cash.

If trader A trades his property for common stock with a readily determinable market value on the day of the trade, he is subject to taxation during the year of the trade. He is in the capital gains area, but he does not attain deferred tax status. It's an unlike trade, and the precise market value of what he received can be readily determined. Appraisal values of various kinds of property including objects of art and antiques vary and are not precise. You have some flexibility with this kind of property.

Moonlight Fortune Tip (MFT) 19
A trader keeps what he gets in trades by
engaging in nontaxable trades.

When a trade involves a cash boot, the trader paying the boot is "trading up," and the other trader is "trading down." The up-trader had no immediate tax liability. The down-trader has tax liability if he has made a determinable profit. If he has paid considerably more cash into the property than the boot he receives, the profit is not readily determinable till he sells the new property. In this case tax liability might be deferred. In this instance, and in most property trade situations, get an interpretation from your accountant.

Every moonlight fortune builder needs a good accountant who knows income tax law. Pick one who's more than a number juggler. He should have a broad knowledge of business, investment, and of course, tax law. If you have an accountant friend who's employed by a business, he probably moonlights by keeping books, filing tax returns, and advising on tax matters. He'll give you more personal attention and he'll give you a break on the cost of your accounting service. You can reciprocate by letting him in on good deals. Both of you will profit from frequent talk sessions.

How to pick your accountant, what he can do for your venture programs, and his role in controlling your growth are covered in Chapter 11. Meanwhile, put MFT 20 in your pocket to help you fatten your wallet.

> *Moonlight Fortune Tip (MFT) 20*
> Get a good accountant. Use his services to
> help shape, enlarge, and control your ven-
> tures for highest profit and lowest tax cost.

HOW TO NEGOTIATE PROFITABLE TRADES

Although the trader's operation involves a considerable amount of pure barter and the medium is generally a property or a product rather than cash, cash is frequently involved in his deals. The trader must reduce property to cash value in order to see that he is making a good deal. Therefore, before you enter into negotiations, you'll want to reduce the other fellow's trade to a cash value within your mind and be sure that the cash value of his trade plus his boot is more valuable on the resale market than the value of your trade. If the trade is the other way around, the resale value of what you get still must exceed the value of what you give. Then, when you start negotiating, start at a greater difference than the difference value that you've established as the smallest profit trading point.

In negotiating for a property or a product, always do more listening than talking. During the course of the conversation, the other trader may emphasize or let slip some of the negatives of the particular item that he is trading. He'll also tip you on his objectives—*what he wants.* When you have determined the benefits that he wants or a way to shape the trade so that his benefits are increased, you're on the way to a working deal. Whenever you talk, build the value of your product in the direction of benefits to him. Build value by appealing to his emotions. In this way, you add intangible value for the other party and the trade is more likely to come off.

Don't be too hasty to revise your trade figure. Make the other party feel that they have really accomplished something under very difficult odds whenever you budge off your initial trade difference. Remember the objective is to make a trade and to make a trade at a profit. If the trading proceeds in a direction that makes it impossible to trade at a profit, you'll have to break off negotiations. However, don't be premature in this respect. The next section will get into the matter of keeping trade deals open and avoiding negotiation cutoffs. I've seen many deals that finally came off in from three days to a year because one of the traders kept the door to a trade open.

If it looks as though you may be heading for an impasse and you can't budge the other party, you might reconfigure the trading package. For example, you might put up another property or another product or even several of these for the property or product that you're trying to trade for. You might also consider concessions and adjustments that can be made in the method of financing or the method of paying the boot which really doesn't cost you any actual cash money. By adjusting and by giving in on minor points, you can generally accomplish the big thing that you wanted to accomplish in your deal.

HOW I NEGOTIATED A $10,000 REDUCTION IN DOWN PAYMENT

Here's how I negotiated a $42,500 property buy (where the seller wanted $12,325 down and a 40-month payout), until the final terms were: a $2,000 cash outlay, a 1-month interest holiday, and an 85-month payout. The seller stated his demands firmly. The realtor said he wouldn't budge. Here are the steps I took to make the deal:

1. I told the realtor I couldn't pay that kind of money down, and I suggested he let me talk to the seller.

2. I met privately with the seller and reviewed my qualifications and my past performance. This built his confidence in me and was a prelude to the credit request that I eventually had to make.

3. I reviewed the seller's age, investment, and income posture in general terms. He was in his early sixties. He and his wife were still earning ordinary unsheltered income (which I mentally estimated in the $15,000-a-year range). He wanted to semi-retire within a year, and I estimated that his unsheltered ordinary income would be halved.

4. I told him I could prepare three deals from which to select that would increase his net proceeds after taxes. (I estimated his net to be approximately $6,000 greater by these methods.) He told me to do it.

5. He had the propositions reviewed by his lawyer, his accountant, his banker, and a businessman friend. They all agreed that he'd net considerably more from any of my proposals than he would from his original proposal.

6. The deal he chose was this:

I would pay him $40,000 net, $2,500 down, the balance over seven years.

I would pay the realtor's commission.

The first month was to be interest-free with payments starting the second month.

7. Rent prorations reduced my payment to him at closing to about $2,000.

8. I gave the realtor a noninterest bearing note for his commission.

Note that I didn't haggle over price. The price was fair, and I needed credit concessions from the seller. I got these because I showed him how the credit concession would increase his interest income and save him tax dollars. I got him cash at closing by separating the realtor's fee and agreeing to pay it. Then I got an additional credit concession by giving the realtor a contract signed by the seller and myself which gave the realtor $150 a month for 16 months simply by signing my name. He wanted cash and was reluctant to deal at first, but he came around quickly when he realized it was the only way the deal would be made.

> *Moonlight Fortune Tip (MFT) 21*
> To negotiate profitable trades, study the other trader's situation. Show him how he gets more by trading on your terms. Show him benefits!

> *Moonlight Fortune Tip (MFT) 22*
> Reduce cash outlay and increase leverage by separating costs and parlaying them into additional credit.

HOW TO KEEP TRADE DEALS OPEN AND AVOID NEGOTIATION CUTOFFS

Sometimes during a negotiation, one or both of the parties tend to become emotional. The trader may cast aspersions on the other trader's mentality, his product, or his offer. When you're on the receiving end, just let it roll off your back and continue to negotiate. If you feel yourself becoming incensed with the attitude of the other trader or feel that he's trying to trade unrealistically hard, don't let yourself get riled. Always end your discussion with, "Well, let's talk about it another time." Always leave the deal open, because if you close it on a harsh word, it may be impossible to ever open it again.

Moonlight Fortune Tip (MFT) 23
Keep the deal open regardless of how far
apart you and the other party are. Avoid
emotional upsets and deal cordially.

It takes time to think out the terms of a deal in each man's
mind. It takes longer for the parties in a deal to communicate
their views on the deal to each other. After communicating, each
of the parties may still require time to accept or develop counter-
offers in a final negotiation.

A trade deal of any magnitude usually requires negotiation.
The negotiation goes smoother if both parties participate. Work
out several workable approaches on paper, but don't take the
paper to the negotiating sessions. Then work it out on paper with
the other party, letting him contribute inputs. Participation by
the other party is essential to a smooth negotiation. Work minor
points on which you'll be willing to yield into the negotiation.
The discussion of these points tends to steer negotiation away
from major points. Hence, there is participation and heavy negotiation on minor issues. It's always better to yield on minor issues
and retain the principal features of the deal.

Moonlight Fortune Tip (MFT) 24
Inject minor issues on which you're willing
to yield into the deal to retain important features.

HOW TO REAP BIG PROFITS IN "APPLES-AND-ORANGES" (UNLIKE) TRADES

The big-time trader knows that he can usually make bigger
profits by trading unlike pieces of property and products. A man
who has a dissatisfaction with the income performance or attention required by a piece of property or a product that he owns
may want to reinvest his equity in another form of property or
product. He sometimes undervalues what he's trying to get rid of,
and he is sometimes already conditioned to make a sacrifice. If

you have the different thing that he's looking for, he tends to value what you have much more highly than the property with which he's displeased. There's opportunity for excellent profits when you discover a situation of this kind.

Another factor which recommends unlike trades is the diversification potential which may accrue to you. The more diversification that you have without dilution of your span of control, the better off you are as a big-time money-maker. Diversification can provide hedges and other advantages which were noted in an earlier chapter.

THE SECRETS OF FINDING SPECIAL SITUATIONS

The special situation is the trader's way of life. If you can find properties or products that involve special situations, such as estate settlements, bankrupt operations, buildings undergoing modernization or destruction, disinterested heirs, or businesses for sale under book value, you can usually make a much more profitable trade. Typical special situations that traders look for include unprofitable businesses that can be converted to profitable businesses, run-down properties that can be upgraded easily, impending divorces, property owned by older persons who are ready to bow out, owners in bad health, or pressing external financial commitments.

For example, one apartment house that I own was obtained from an absentee owner who just couldn't get good management into the property. I've obtained automobiles from people at attractive prices when they got tired of them and didn't want to devote much effort to selling them.

I know a fellow in the used furniture business who keeps his eye open for divorce situations. When he hears of such a situation, he goes to the residence, indicates that he is in the used furniture business, passes his card, and indicates that he'll be glad to buy any or all of the furniture if they decide to refurbish the house. He also keeps his eye open for houses that are for sale on the off chance that a divorce may be in process or that the owner will dispose of some of the things that he has.

> *Moonlight Fortune Tip (MFT) 25*
> Look for special situations. They're gen-
> erally the fountainhead of opportunity.

THE SPECIAL INFORMATION TECHNIQUES THAT MAKE BIG PROFIT TRADES

You'll be a much more effective trader if you develop lines of communication that make special information available to you. Take advantage of the information gathering and forecasting techniques discussed in this book to build a base. Expand this base constantly through routine research and special information gathering.

Much of your special information will come to you from friends who are knowledgeable in various aspects of the business world, from friends who have close contacts with local, state, and national government, and through your other day-to-day associations. In addition, you can acquire a large amount of information which will influence your trading by keeping track of the *Wall Street Journal,* business magazines, and the daily newspapers. You'll also obtain information from special service reports that you can subscribe to, from local Chambers of Commerce, and published government reports and figures. Keep your ear to the ground and you'll find more good deals than you can possibly handle.

The classified sections of city newspapers are bonanzas of special business information and new opportunities. I contend that a man starting with about $1,000 who studies the classifieds full-time and makes penetrating phone inquiries can make $50,-000 a year or more simply by trading and providing services. It's riskier to do it full-time without a good base, but a no-risk moonlighter can still make good money at it. As an exercise, try it out with today's paper. You'll probably emerge with a deal, and you'll pick up a good bit of new business-opportunity knowledge.

> *Moonlight Fortune Tip (MFT) 26*
> Develop a good information base and stay
> on the path of opportunity by developing
> communication lines to special opportunity
> situations.

VISION MAXIMIZES TRADE PROFITS

Every successful businessman and resourceful trader attempts to base his present and future judgments on past history and prevailing trends. The advent of the automobile, for example, created a large number of related industries. When the automobile was in its infancy, roads were poor and limited. There were opportunities for service stations, garages, and the numerous automobile services that I'll discuss in Chapter 9. Many smart men got in on the ground floor by sewing up profitable dealerships. Many of them took dealerships in towns where they knew the business would be unprofitable initially. They were betting on the future. This kind of vision has made many a fortune.

The big-time trader is finely tuned to economic trends. He can sense when recession or boom looms ahead. He sells and trades at high prices during periods of boom. During periods of recession, he buys at low prices. The trader who deals in the stock market sells when prices are high and buys when prices are down. A trader tries to time his borrowing so that he borrows short-term money during periods of boom and invests it during periods of recessions. He repays his loans during the following boom period. He does not secure long-term loans when he can avoid it during boom periods when interest rates are high. He reserves his long-term borrowing for periods of recession when interest rates are generally low.

Certain businesses may be up while other businesses are down. The trader amasses trading material in the industries that are down and divests himself of property in businesses that are on the boom. The trader keeps his eye open for special events which can affect his market. In the stock market, he buys on bad news when prices are down and sells on good news when prices are up. Vision and timing are among the trader's most valuable talents.

> *Moonlight Fortune Tip* (*MFT*) 27
> Develop your vision and timing sense to capitalize on new developments, economic trends, and changing mores.

ARBITRAGE—THE SPECIAL HORIZON

Arbitrage is defined as "the simultaneous purchase and sale of the same securities, commodities, or foreign exchange in different markets to profit from unequal prices." There's a lot of profit to be made in arbitrage. An arbitrager is generally not a local operator. He operates in markets scattered all over the United States and abroad as well. Prior to a merger of companies, there frequently is an arbitrage situation in the value between the two stocks. The arbitrager buys the stock that has the price advantage and sells the other stock short. He replaces the shorted stock with his purchased stock on delivery. Hence, the proceeds of the short sale minus the cost of his long purchase is his profit.

Since the values of various properties, commodities, and products exist in men's minds and since these values can be different from mind to mind, the trader is basically an arbitrager who collapses longer periods of time into relatively short periods of time. That is, he buys today from one man at a lower price because the value of the article is at a lower price in the man's mind and he sells to another man tomorrow at a higher price because that other man holds a higher value for the product in his mind. If he had contacted and sold the second man today, he would have probably gotten the same price; so basically, since the transaction of purchase and sale is ordinarily not consummated by three parties simultaneously, the arbitrager utilizes varying time spans in his definition of simultaneous purchase and sale.

There's a potential arbitrage situation in silver coins. The weight of silver in these coins has an actual value that exceeds the face value of the coins. It's illegal to smelt silver coins. Nevertheless, speculators are collecting and buying silver coins against the possibility that the law may be changed or that the government may repurchase coins above face value. Since the introduction of sandwich coins in the mid-sixties, silver coins have been disappearing from circulation at a rapid rate. This has been brought about by the speculation cited. It is fostered by the fact that a speculator can take coins to the bank as collateral and get a 100 percent loan.

> *Moonlight Fortune Tip (MFT) 28*
> Keep your eyes open for arbitrage opportunities. Small percentage advantages taken in volume produce large profits.

WHERE FORTUNES ARE BEING MADE IN TRADING

In Charles Morrow Wilson's book *Let's Try Barter*,[1] he relates a number of interesting stories about small-scale bartering. Any moonlight trader will find this book interesting and is sure to glean some interesting ideas from it. For example, Wilson tells about a dentist who bartered dental work for most of the cost of a new house; of a widow who acquired luxuries as well as many of the necessities of life by trading piano lessons; he tells of barter shops that were set up by some enterprisers. Incidentally, one of these shops engaged in heavy trading of duplicate or unwanted wedding presents.

Lots of money has been made in trading coins and stamps. Speculation in uncirculated rolls and silver adds to the profit fire.

---

[1] Published by Devin-Adair Co., New York, 1960.

One of my friends trades in paintings, another in antiques. Much of the latter's business is generated with women to whom he has sold antiques who become tired of them after a while and bring them back to trade for other antiques. Automobile trading is big business. Trading of specialized hobby equipment such as boats, ham radio equipment, and sporting equipment is another business possibility that you may want to investigate.

The stock market of course is one of the biggest trader businesses in all the world. I've tried to limit my references to the stock market and to stock as a means of accumulating wealth since numerous books have been written on this subject and I'd like to defer to those.

The commodity market offers tremendous opportunities for trade profits. The leverage is good, and a competent trader can make substantial profits. Inexperienced traders can take a bad beating, too. Before you plunge, research it in the library and follow it with "make-believe" trades for a while. Locate some traders and benefit from their experience and savvy. Then, try it with real money!

TRADE AROUND THE WORLD TODAY—
TOMORROW THROUGH OUTER SPACE

World trade has always been attractive to American businessmen. It's attractive for a number of reasons: First of all, the growth in backward countries tends to open new markets and create opportunities for American companies. The products that are produced in backward countries are generally produced at lower cost than they can be in the United States. Many of these products have faraway, romantic values that are sought by Americans. Consequently, they're in demand and yet they can be sold at attractive prices in the United States. This has attracted large numbers of American businesses (ranging from individuals with limited resources to large corporations) into import-export and overseas ventures.

A good way to start to get into world trade is to enter the import-export business on a small scale. It isn't difficult and you don't have to buy an expensive course to get started. Write to the Chamber of Commerce of the United States (the Foreign Policy Department) and order a copy of their book, *Import and Export Business,* a neat 130-page book that gives you the hard facts of running your own import-export business. The address of the United States Chamber of Commerce is: 1615 H Street, NW, Washington, D. C. This book discusses methods of importing through indirect and direct purchasing, organizing for direct import, how to place an import order, financing imports, custom procedures, export trading and methods, analysis of export opportunities, how to handle an export order, financing reports, advertising, and foreign trade restrictions. This book has been available in the past at $2.00, and it is one of the best bargains that I know of.

Once you've established yourself in the import-export business on a small scale, you'll soon expand into bigger things. One of my friends started in the import-export business in his spare time. Within a matter of two years, he had retired from his job and now spends all his time importing and exporting. I believe he works no more than three hours a day but he lives very well on that.

7

DISCOVER YOUR RESOURCES: THE SECRETS OF CONVERTING JUNK, FREE RESOURCES, AND UNRECOGNIZED CAPABILITIES INTO VALUABLE ASSETS

THE RAW MATERIALS OF MONEY-MAKING

Resources are the raw materials of money-making. Resources are things that the money-maker can convert into cash or use to convert other resources into cash. Resources may be material, machinery, test equipment, the printed page, cash, the ability to borrow, a hobby, a skill, raw materials, land, buildings, manpower, or mindpower. Virtually anything that can be used to produce something or that can be converted into something that people are willing to pay for is a resource.

This chapter deals with the exploitation of your resources in any business as well as businesses based on direct exploitation of natural resources. You have many resources within yourself, in your home, and elsewhere which you may not be aware of. It is the purpose of this chapter to help you discover these hidden resources.

HOW TO HARNESS A HOST OF MILLION- AND BILLION-DOLLAR MACHINES—FREE

There are a host of million- and billion-dollar machines that you can harness to build your moonlight fortune. The first one is really close to home—it's you. The others are close at hand, too.

You are of course much more than a machine. Since we human beings convert energy and do work, it's productive to analyze ourselves as machines. We're very flexible machines and we possess capabilities that mechanical machines cannot duplicate. We're flesh, bones, mind, and individuals with feelings, sensitivities and unique characteristics. Let's take a quick inventory of your human resources.

Your human resources include: your mind which generates ideas that may be converted directly into cash; your eyes and ears which pick up information for use as a mental catalyst as well as information that you can resell; your hands which write, type, and enable you to perform delicate design and manufacturing operations. Your physical appearance is a resource because it can help you to impress people favorably and thereby enhance your chances of gaining their support in your projects. Your speech and the way you express yourself is another important resource because it enables you to win people to your point of view and to muster their support for your projects and as customers. Your legs are resources because through them you can move from place to place where opportunity awaits you. It's too bad that so few people realize the tremendous potential that they have within their own body and use it so poorly. If you can harness your human resources fully, you can experience 1,000 to 10,000 percent more success in everything that you undertake. My book on the subject of success will help you to capitalize fully on these resources.[1]

Your human resources, their development, and their exploitation, are the basis of the most powerful *Moonlight Fortune* capability of all. Mark MFT 29 as the key to everything!

> *Moonlight Fortune Tip (MFT) 29*
> Your personal human resources have bound-less potential. Develop them to their utmost and use them wisely to accelerate your fortunes.

Now, what about those million- and billion-dollar machines that you can harness free?

I've talked about some of them in earlier chapters. The U.S. Government is one of them. Through loans, subsidies, available research, publications, and advisory services, the U.S. Government puts a machine of information-diggers and disseminators, statisticians, scientists, financiers, and "angels" at your disposal. All you have to do to harness this machine and its many peripherals is to follow the advice and pointers in this book. Investigate the agencies cited in earlier chapters. Find what they have to offer that may be helpful to you. As a starter, you have the vast resources of the U.S. Government Printing Office at your disposal. To probe further into the U.S. Government and what it can do for you, get a copy of the U.S. Government Organization Manual, available from the Government Printing Office. When you make more money, Uncle Sam collects more income taxes. It's common sense that Uncle profits when he helps.

Chambers of Commerce publish maps, directories of manufacturers, retailers, and other businesses. These provide location information, planning information and prospect and source lists. In the larger cities, a specialist devoted to the various interests of

---

[1] Miracle Success System: A Scientific Way to Get What You Want out of Life (West Nyack, N.Y.: Parker Publishing Co., Inc., 1967.)

the Chamber stands ready to help you in any matter. The larger Chambers have a research department that stands ready to answer inquiries. If the Chamber can help you establish a business, the community benefits. That's the Chamber's job.

MORE "MACHINES" TO HELP YOU

Trade and professional associations can help you, too. There are published directories of trade and professional associations. Check your library for it. These associations employ full-time directors who know their field well. Many of these associations have regular periodical publications. They'll provide information and direction that will help you in pursuing specific business fields.

The libraries, and I emphasize this by repetition, are bonanza machines. They include your local town library, large city libraries, college and university libraries, and the U.S. Library of Congress. If you'll learn how to milk them, they'll be more productive than the largest dairy herd in the world—not with milk—with money!

Now, let's get back to the best machine of all—you!

You possess additional resources that cannot be counted directly in dollars. These resources are the skill that you have acquired and utilized in the performance of your regular job and the skills that you acquired in your earlier working career. Walter Chrysler pyramided skills that he acquired while working in the railroad shops into the Chrysler Corporation.

Another set of resources that are generally not counted in dollars are resources that you have acquired in the pursuit of hobbies and other interests. Joe S. was interested in ham radio and began to repair radios in his spare time. When television came in, he learned how to repair television sets. Today he owns one of the largest television dealerships in the United States. John L. fell in love with automobiles while he was in high school. He began by making repairs on his own automobile and soon found himself repairing the automobiles of his friends. By the time he graduated from high school, he was ready to go into his own garage business with the money he had made moonlighting while in high school. Today he has a large Chevrolet dealership.

> *Moonlight Fortune Tip (MFT) 30*
> The world is full of money-making machines that you can harness free. They include governments, Chambers of Commerce, associations, and libraries. They operate on the simple premise that by helping you, they help themselves. Everywhere along the line you'll find yourself operating in a similar fashion.

BOTTOMLESS SOURCES OF SPECIALIZED
MONEY-MAKING SKILLS

In early 1969, I determined through a quick informal survey of some 50 friends and associates making $20,000 a year or more in their basic jobs that:

1. 70 percent of them were engaged in moonlight activities ranging from simple services to complex investment activities.

2. Another 20 percent wished they were making moonlight money but couldn't figure out how to start or were afraid to try.

3. The remaining 10 percent didn't care to try because they were happy with their incomes, had inherited side incomes, or would become heirs.

Supervisory-level and technician-level people have always sought moonlight income. They're available and they'll do comparatively good work at reasonably low pay when you consider that you're paying only for actual production.

Hence, you can profit in your moonlight endeavors by hiring moonlighters. Sources of moonlight labor, management, and specialty talents are adequate to meet your demands.

Moonlight Fortune Tip (MFT) 31
Staff your moonlight ventures with moonlighters. That way you pay for direct work
only.

Other sources of specialized money-making skills are available
to you, and in this case on a no-cost basis, through the numerous "machines" cited in the preceding section.

WEALTH ON THE EARTH

Wealth exists on the earth in the form of vegetation—food
plants, flowers, trees, and other plants convertible to useful
products. There is wealth in owning and using the land itself, and
even the view, general environment, or access to other assets—
such as water for industry or for transportation—has value. The
animal life on the land and the ability of the land to support
animal life has value.

How do you tap the national resources of the land? One time-
honored approach is to buy acreage, harvest the tree crop, and
keep it planted as a tree farm till it pays for itself and appreciates
in value. Another traditional approach is to clear the land, sell
the lumber harvest, and then develop the land into agricultural
acreage till the city grows to it. Then the land is sold at an
appreciated price.

Vacation and weekend retreats with ultimate resort potential
have long been part of the dreams of many Americans. The
dream is becoming more realistic as rural acreage becomes
scarcer and scarcer. At the present rate of population and industrial growth, country atmosphere and "places to get away
from it all" will be very scarce in 30 years. Hence, an investment
in a country place of considerable acreage now will have considerable resort value—if you don't succumb to the urge to take
appreciation profit from a developer in the interim. So much for
the ground itself.

Farming and ranching has become big business. The small

farmer or rancher has a hard life and a low income. The gentleman weekend farmer or rancher may possibly lose his tax shelter in the near future through impending tax reform. Unless you want to go at farming in a big way, steer clear of it if your only interest is profit. If you enjoy it and get hobby-fun out of it, it can help to pay off the property, though it cannot earn at the accelerated rate of other investments.

Tree farming is not a big-profit business. It will pay for low-cost acreage under long-term finance. See your County Agent and write the U.S. Department of Agriculture (USDA) for information on how-to-do-it and for the state and federal governmental aids available to you on agricultural tree-farming and ranching ventures. There are numerous subsidies and loans available for these ventures. Some states have special financing arrangements and grants for veterans who want to farm.

Although bodies of water and their potential will be discussed in the next section, a few comments are in order here. If you buy land with all of a pond or lake on it, it's yours unless there are deed restrictions. Large lakes and ponds suitable for recreational purposes enhance the value of the surrounding land. If you buy river or lakefront property, you may or may not have exclusive rights to the use of your frontage. In some cases governments and municipalities retain easements on the frontage. Check this out before you buy.

Flowers have become big business in the USA. Most flowers which are sold commercially are hothouse grown. Some flowers and plants are grown for use in medicines and for food seasoning. If you have an interest in flowers, pour a little research into the subject. You may find an outlet for your hobby that is more profitable than growing flowers for decoration or special occasion remembrances. USDA or your county agent may be able to help you.

The animal wealth on the land, domesticated and wild, offers opportunity. Animal meat supplied from domesticated animals on efficient ranches provides our food mainstay. But domestic animals have other uses. Horses are used for show, race, and riding recreation. Small animals become pets. There's plenty of profit in these fields if you have the knowledge to reap it. Wild animals bred on hunting refuges are becoming more valuable as they are being driven from land devoted to other uses. "Deer leases" are common in Texas and in some other states. The "shooting preserve" is becoming common in many parts of the country. If you like the outdoors and hunting, check the possibilities. It may not make you filthy rich immediately, but it will help you pay for the land, and someday that will make you rich.

RICHES IN THE AIR

The riches in the air are in their early stages of exploitation. They had their beginning with the hunter who shot wild fowl for food in our country's early history. But till the advent of the plane and passenger routes, the air was not considered valuable. Hence, in the late '20's and early '30's, less than 50 years ago, the concept of air routes, the right to use them and their value as a dollar asset were first realized. They have become the basic asset essential to the large air-transportation industry.

The value of the air (and we're still really talking only about space over the ground) became apparent again in a new use during the last two decades as urban congestion made downtown land scarce. The concept of "air rights," the right to erect a structure beginning a number of feet above a piece of land was thus born. Air rights can be bought to erect buildings over roads, bodies of water, and other features. The concept will continue to expand as the population and modern technology grow.

But, there's value in air for an even more fundamental reason—the fact that we breathe it! For most of this nation's history, clean, pure breathing air was available almost everywhere.

Then, with the advent of industry a process of air pollution began around the industrial towns. The automobile made further inroads on the pure air. Today we face a pollution crisis. The Department of Transportation is pushing for nonpolluting vehicles. The Department of Health, Education and Welfare is pushing for more stringent pollution controls.

There will be countless fortunes made in anti-pollution devices, nonpolluting manufacturing processes, and a complete change in our concept of transportation which presently uses internal combustion engines. The internal combustion engine will be replaced by external combustion engines which will reduce pollutants by a factor of almost 10. This change will literally do away with the concept of automobile engines, filling stations, and garages as we now know them. There are fortunes to be made here, not from this natural resource, but from the equipment and businesses needed to keep the air clean.

FORTUNES IN THE RIVERS AND THE SEAS

There are eleven definable large industries associated with the ocean. A number of these have application to rivers, lakes, and other inland bodies of water. Some of these industries have been thriving for years. Many of them are in the pioneering stages and hence present unusual opportunities. Here are the 11 ocean/water industries:

1. *Recreation and Pleasure*—People will always want to enjoy the water. This includes boating, fishing, surfing, swimming, travel, and other hobby-sport pursuits. There are markets for manufacturing, services, and sales. The opportunities for trading are great.

2. *Extraction of Petroleum and Drilling*—Exploration, drilling, and production of gas and oil are big business. Exploration and mining of minerals on and beneath the ocean floor is an emerging horizon. Look for transportation of oil, minerals, and

marine food through water pipelines to processing areas ashore.

3. *Water Purification*—Rapid consumption and pollution of inland waters opens the door wide for purification methods and equipment for both inland waters and the sea. Sea water requires desalting as well.

4. *Chemicals from Water*—Processing water to extract minerals in solution and in the case of sea water to extract other minerals, chemicals, marine and plant life for industrial chemicals and pharmaceuticals offers many possibilities.

5. *Transportation*—Ships, crew boats, tugs, tankers, freighters and run-abouts are needed for transporting men and materials to ocean work-sites as well as for the regular travel and shipping trades as we think of them. Special submersible vehicles will be required for undersea activity. Designers, builders, and operators take profit in this business.

6. *Underwater Construction*—Development, design, and construction of undersea structures will be big business. These structures will be required for undersea work, exploration, and living. This is another big future horizon.

7. *Marine Salvage*—The salvage value of sunken vessels, structures, and cargo is pegged in the billions of dollars. Some of these prizes lie at depths that have made salvage impossible or uneconomical with available technology. Recent technical breakthroughs have made salvage of many of these sunken prizes practical. As technology advances, more charted prizes will be recovered and uncharted ones discovered. If you're interested, start with the *Encyclopaedia Britannica,* and then work the Public Library. Also try the U.S. Maritime Commission, Washington, D. C. If you're adventure minded and willing to work hard, this may be your cup of tea.

8. *Food from the Sea*—The location, harvesting, and processing of marine life and plants for food will become a bigger and more highly technical business. The harvest of the sea will provide food for humans and animals as well as soil fertilizer.

9. *Power Generation*—The tides, waves, winds, currents, and temperature differentials in the ocean are potential sources of commercial energy. There's wealth in it for those who can find the means to harness this energy.

10. *Science and Technological Services*—A whole new industry provides research, specialized services, instrumentation, systems, and equipment needed by other ocean industries. Again, if you're a technical man, here's a big new horizon.

11. *Military and Government*—The U.S. Government has a vast stake in the oceans for defense, information, and services to the American ocean industry and U.S. citizens. Submarine, anti-submarine and other undersea warfare techniques provide large challenges and large markets. Weather services, coast services, and geodetic surveys require new techniques, new equipments, and new services.

If you're interested in learning more about the opportunities of the oceans, pursue the basic research that I've recommended. In addition, you may wish to subscribe to some of the ocean-ography magazines. One of the better ones is:

Ocean Industry
Gulf Publishing Company
P. O. Box 2608
Houston, Texas 77001

Another wonderful source of background is the National Geographic Society. Check up on articles they've run over the last 10 or 15 years in *National Geographic*.

BIG TIME FORTUNES IN SALVAGE AND DISPOSAL

There are fortunes in scraps. Ben Fixman raised eyebrows when he predicted in 1963 that his company would be doing $200 million in sales in five years. At the time, his company was doing only about $6 million a year. His prediction was correct, and in 1968 he predicted that his company would be doing more than a $1 billion by 1971.

Fixman founded his company, Diversified Metals, in 1956. He had lost his shirt on a previous try in the scrap-metal business, but he didn't give up. He felt that the secret to success was a method for separating wire from insulation without heat. Burning produces air pollution. A "no-heat" process (which would not produce pollution) would release a large reservoir of raw materials in old insulated telephone, railroad, and utility wire lines. It took Fixman two years to solve the puzzle. He developed a mechanical process that grinds up the scrap wire without heat and spits out pure copper and aluminum pellets. He guards the proprietary details. In 1968 he had three plants with a fourth under construction.

One of the by-products of the American way of life is waste. Every day millions of dollars worth of slightly used and perhaps slightly damaged products or reclaimable products are thrown out in the trash-can, burned or pushed down the drain. Goodwill Industries developed a way for employing handicapped people in repairing this reclaimed and highly usable waste. Another business which uses a valuable and frequently discarded resource is the used bookstore.

Old clothes, collected and bundled, are exported to the poorer nations of the world where they bring great joy to the people who have never worn anything quite so fine. And all along the way, there are people who are making profit on the transactions.

There's money in waste paper, too. One resourceful young man in Dallas, Texas, bought a shredder. He collects old newspapers, runs them through the shredder, and sells the shredded paper for packing material.

Another Dallas man is in the house-wrecking business. He wrecks houses and clears the interiors of buildings that are to be remodeled. He gets paid for this, and the revenue more than covers expenses. Then he sells the salvage for additional profits. He has a good foreman to supervise the jobs and he has a roster of moonlighters and retired men to staff his work crews. In addition, he operates a used lumber and salvage yard where he also sells paint and other new hardware.

BIG TIME FORTUNES IN RESOURCES—AROUND THE WORLD

Less developed countries usually have abundant natural resources and cheap labor. They need business management, production capabilities, and education and skills training for their citizens. If you have a job that causes you to live in a foreign country or travel to it, you can explore the possibilities and get a venture going. Airline pilots find overseas moonlight ventures exciting and profitable. If you're interested in exploring the possibilities, you might start by requesting information on specific countries from the U.S. State Department. The government of the country of interest can also supply information. Get general background on the country in the *Encyclopaedia Britannica* and other information source books.

HOW TO UNCOVER HIDDEN MONEY AND PUT IT TO WORK

Most of the excuses you hear from the people who never made it, boil down to, "I didn't have the money to get started," or "I don't have the capital I need."

Baloney!

I've already cited numerous ventures that can be started without any cash whatsoever. Admittedly, you can grow your fortune faster if you have some cash to help your program along. The fundamental resources—men, money, materials, machines and plant—tied together by the basic success-producing resource —management—available in adequate quantity and proportion, ease the ascent to wealth. So, let's inventory your cash resources and uncover hidden bonanzas and means to build a starter's stack of chips.

Remember those U.S. Savings Bonds that you've been buying over the years? You may have several thousand dollars' worth of these bonds in your possession right now. You don't even need to cash them to get working cash. You can use them as loan collateral.

What about your insurance policies? If you'll check your insurance policies, you'll find that they have cash values. You can usually borrow the cash value of the policy at low interest rates from the insurance company.

Another cash resource that many people overlook is the equity in their homes. Most Americans buy their homes for anything from a few hundred dollars to several thousand dollars down, and borrow the balance. The amount that you paid into your home over the years plus the appreciation that you have had due to rising prices of labor and land represents your equity in your home. You can either sell it, place a second lien on it (that is, borrow money and give a second lien against the property), or you can refinance it with a new first lend. Consequently, you can pull the cash difference between what the property is worth and what is now owed for any investment that you may wish to make.

Your automobile is another asset. If your automobile is clear, then you can use it as collateral to borrow at your bank. If you need a car in your moonlight ventures (and you usually do), the mere fact that you have one reduces start-up cash requirements.

What about your attic? Have you checked your attic, garage, or your storage house lately? You might even find valuable antiques. At any rate, you'll find a lot of things that can be sold through a rummage or garage sale. Perhaps you'll find tools or materials that you'll be able to use directly in your new ventures.

Do you have any collections that you're willing to sell or put up as loan collateral? That stamp, coin, or what-have-you collection that you started as a youth and have long since abandoned may provide just the nest egg you need to get started.

Those stocks and bonds that you bought years ago and forgot about because they became valueless—check up on them. They may be worth something now. Stocks and bonds may be sold for cash or used as loan collateral. If you buy stocks through a company option, you don't need to break the three-year hold to pull cash. Simply borrow on them.

Do you have a piece of property somewhere that's not being used productively? Sell it, or borrow against it. Turn it into a cash-flow producer as well. Perhaps you own part of a property as a result of an inheritance. Sell your part to the other heirs, or buy out the other heirs on unsecured notes and refinance or sell the property. Be sure you can meet the payments on both obligations though!

What about Aunt Mary or Uncle Harry? Can you borrow money from them? Keep family borrowing on a business basis though!

What about loans you've made to relatives or friends? Can you collect on them now? Or do you hold any notes that you can collect on by offering a discount?

What about the government-backed loans cited earlier?

There's money (or resources convertible to money) around in abundance. Loan money goes through alternations of easy lending and tight lending. Economists alternately and concurrently talk inflation and deflation. One financial advisor says, "Borrow and speculate; there's inflation ahead." Another says, "Be conservative; your dollar will buy more in a few years."

One thing is sure: The long-term trend is inflationary. Inflation is built into the American economy. There'll be some downs with the general "up" trend, but the moonlighter has more built-in protection than the full-time investor or the full-time job holder who's not a moonlighter. People who become rich do so during boom and bust. Some others become less rich. Set up a good plan with hedges for either eventuality, and then make it work for you.

There's cash around. Put it to work.

HOW TO GET A FACTORY—FREE

In Chapter 2 I told you how to get office and factory space with no cash or a very minimal cash outlay. There are other possibilities if you want to start a larger operation.

Many towns trying to bolster their economies have bought or erected factories for companies during the last four decades. There was a splurge in community-owned factories leased to new industries that began after World War II, particularly in the South. The community sought out industry to move into the town. They generally offered tax benefits, adequate manpower at low cost, and low-rent, long-term leases on factories. The community bought and refurbished old factories or built new ones from the ground up. They financed the factories through bond issues. (Communities can readily place long-term bond issues if the voters approve because municipal bonds are tax exempt and hence appeal to high-income earners.) In some cases the communities bought surplus Federal properties (old military camps and bases) for this purpose.

Generally this requires a business that is large in terms of what starting moonlight fortune builders can afford—50 or more employees. But, there are exceptions and special cases. There are a number of old towns that are retrogressing. Many of these have old vacant buildings that will serve nicely as factories after minor refurbishment. Abundant and low-cost labor is usually available in these towns. If you find one of these towns you may be able to put a package together that will get you a factory at low rent with an option to buy, by providing employment for as few as five or ten people at the start. Think about this one if you're considering a manufacturing venture!

Training subsidies and the push to make every American employable may help you in finding a low-cost factory, too. The rewards in helping disadvantaged people to become self-sustaining are more than financial. If you're located near a concentrated poverty area or if you're a Negro, you have some special things going for you in getting a start.

HOME RESOURCES MAKE ASTOUNDING FORTUNES

Many a woman has made a fortune with her kitchen stove. There are some men who have been known to use the kitchen stove as capital equipment. One of the earliest Hewlett-Packard test instruments was given an environmental test in the kitchen oven. (David Packard became Deputy Defense Director in 1969.) Many bakeries and catering services have started in home kitchens. Margaret Rudkin started baking bread in her kitchen. Within a year she was selling more than 15,000 loaves a month. The company that evolved from her moonlighting start is famous Pepperidge Farms. Robert Wian of Glendale, California, had his stove in a 10-seat diner. One day a customer asked for something new in a hamburger, so Wian slashed a bun twice, slapped a hamburger patty on each side of the center slice, put cheese on one and then some relish and lettuce on the other, and came up with the Big Boy hamburger. If you haven't eaten a Big Boy hamburger, you're one of the few.

Another resource that can be found in most American homes is the sewing machine. During the past century, more than 40,000 sewing-machine patents have been granted. Consequently, the sewing machine in the modern home is an advanced machine indeed. Many resourceful women have used the sewing machine to start profitable moonlight ventures ranging from mending to custom clothes, clothing factories and designing.

Think about those tools that you have in your tool box or in your workshop. Bob McCullouch, Chairman Emeritus of Ling-Temco-Vought and founder of Temco, came to the United States with a very small amount of money and a tool box. Ling-Temco-Vought is now one of the largest corporations in the United

States with sales at the time of this writing of $3.2 billion a year. Probably that number will have increased substantially by the time this book goes into print.

The kitchen table, an old battered typewriter, and a few dollars were the only resources that Joseph Cossman had when he launched his highly successful mail-order business. Today, Cossman does business that is measured in the millions of dollars. Yet he started it all on a kitchen table.

Perhaps you have a flair for art or for design and drafting. This capability is a resource. So is a drawing board, a T-square, and pencil, paint and brushes.

I know one elderly couple who have made a living for a number of years by doing decoupage and by making unusual lamps.

A young couple whom I know buy rather plain-looking wooden purses and decorate them with all sorts of little travel stickers and what have you. These purses cost about $3.00 in the rough, and when they are finished, they sell for $35.00.

So you see that some of the common things around your house—the very common possessions that you take for granted and use for pleasure or for living—can be put to work in a new business that may mean a new start in life for you and ultimate riches and wealth.

WEALTH BENEATH THE EARTH

Natural resources are wealth under the land, on the land, in the oceans and rivers around the land, and in the space above and beyond the land. Man's first attempts to exploit these resources were made on the land, then in the waters, then under the land, and finally in space.

Many fortunes have been made in minerals and mining. One approach is to prospect for minerals from a base of knowledge. I came across a very interesting book that I believe provides a sound base of mineral knowledge, and I'd like to recommend it to you. It's *Range Guide to Mines and Minerals*,[2] by Jay E. Ransom. This book tells how and where to find valuable ores and minerals in the United States on a state-by-state basis pinpointing counties and actual locations within some of the counties. In addition to this good location information, the book contains an introduction to mining and mineralogy, how to prepare and start your mineral collection, the techniques for prospecting for profit, and how to start a small mine. The author of the book, Mr. Ransom, has written a number of other books that you may want to look into. They include: *Fossils in America*,[3] *The Rock Hunter's Range Guide*,[4] *Arizona Gem Trails*,[5] and *Petrified Forest Trails Field Guide*.[6]

There's a lot of talk about the status of the U.S. dollar and its possible devaluation. This could occur in a number of ways. One possibility is that the price of gold will be repegged above the $35 an ounce level which the U.S. still supported in late 1969. This talk has sparked new interest in mining, because mineral deposits which could not yield on a profitable basis earlier might be profitably mined when metal market values increase. Hence unmined but known low-yield deposits and old abandoned mines could once again become profitable. This has led to speculation in gold and other mineral stocks and to direct investment in abandoned mines and unmined mineral properties.

To obtain a broad base of knowledge on minerals and mining, consult the *Encyclopaedia Britannica*. It contains excellent articles under the titles "mineralogy" and "mining" illustrated with photographs and easy-to-understand sketches. Other articles in the *Britannica* which relate to ore deposits, specific metals, and metallurgy may interest you. To get more detailed information,

---

[2] Published by Harper & Row, Publishers, Inc., New York, 1964.
[3] Published by Harper & Row, Publishers, Inc., New York, 1964.
[4] Published by Harper & Row, Publishers, Inc., New York, 1962.
[5] Published by J. D. Simpson, Spokane, Wash., 1955.
[6] Published by Gembooks, Mentone, Calif.

write to the U.S. Bureau of Mines, Washington, D.C., or to the U.S. Government Printing Office for a list of publications relating to mining.

Thomas Felix Bolack set out to make his fortune at the age of 26 with savings he had accumulated as an oil-field laborer. He set out to make his fortune in oil. For three years he searched for oil across the arroyos of the San Juan basin in northwestern New Mexico and into southwestern Colorado. He put 350,000 miles on his car in his search. He moonlighted in temporary jobs and used his rifle to hunt food for sustenance. His trip started during World War II not far from the Los Alamos atomic facilities. Bolack had an enlarged heart that made him draft exempt. In mid-1946 he began to buy oil leases from the federal government at 25¢ an acre. He put his car up as collateral to obtain a $600 loan with which he bought a 2400-acre lease. Then he began to sell the oil leases to major oil companies. He sold most of his first flock of leases to the Delhi-Taylor Oil Co. for about $20,000. With this $20,000, he bought $14,000 worth of additional basin leases, paid off his old debts, and went back to selling leases at a profit and buying more leases.

At one point, Bolack held or controlled leases on 100,000 acres of basin land. In the late '40's, his hunches on oil and gas began to pay off. El Paso Natural Gas Co. began putting one productive gas well after another in the basin. Everybody was scrambling for his leases. Less than ten years later, his 25¢-an-acre leases were selling for $5,000. By 1951, his net worth was estimated at more than $3,000,000. In 1958, he picked up some 50,000 acres of oil leases in Canada. In 1960, he became Lieutenant-Governor of New Mexico.

Cases of fortune building in oil are numerous and the approaches are multi-faceted. You'll recall the approach to investment through a syndicate cited in Chapter 5. Stock investment is another. If you want to get closer to nature, start your study with *Britannica,* the U.S. Bureau of Mines publications, and your local library.

Other sources of wealth beneath the earth include underground cavities for special projects such as mushroom growing, cavities for transportation and communication (tunnels), and defense shelters. Tunnels are becoming increasingly important as we choke the terrain with roads, tracks, and right-of-ways. High-speed ground transportation of the future moving at speeds of 150 to 300 miles per hour will require the protection from debris afforded by tunnels. If you can invent machinery which cuts tunnels faster and at lower cost, you'll make a tremendous fortune.

8

HOW TO MAKE OUT IN
MANUFACTURING AND CONSTRUCTION

HOW TO DISCOVER OR DEVELOP A PRODUCT
TO MANUFACTURE

The discovery and development of a product to manufacture is relatively easy if you'll keep a few simple concepts in mind. First of all, in order for a product to be saleable, there has to be a market for it. There'll be a market for a product if the product fulfills existing needs, performs a useful service, and can perform the service in a way different from existing products. In other words, people must want the product that you're going to manufacture or it will not be a success. Saleability of the product must be your first criterion.

I'd like to expand on this to be sure that the point sticks in your mind. If your new product will do something better, less expensively, or in a different way, it meets the first criterion of a successful product. Then, if the product is sufficiently different from those on the market to catch the eye of the customer and excite his interest, its saleability is further enhanced. Next, the amount of competition in the field and the ultimate sales potential of all products of its kind must be considered. For example,

145

if you were to attempt to manufacture ball-point pens at a profit, you would have considerably more competition working the market than if you developed a totally new concept in writing instruments with which to enter the market. Consequently, the ball-point pen would be a poorer product choice than a new writing concept which is not available from the large number of competitors in the market.

Suppose that you are interested in the manufacture (construction) of houses and that the present economic situation in your area is such that there is a glut of new and used houses on the market. The community doesn't need or want any additional houses since there is already an available surplus which is unsold.

Another concept to bear in mind in connection with new products is that the product need not be totally new and innovative. Your new product may contain only a minor variation from an existing product so long as this variation provides the feature which makes your product more desirable.

HOW TO CHANGE PRODUCTS FOR PROFIT

Consider existing products and give them some thought. How can you change them in order to create a new market? For example, can you make the product bigger, smaller, longer, shorter, wider? Can you make it lighter, heavier, or stronger? Can you make it faster or slower? Can you change its shape?

Perhaps you can change the color or make it multicolored. Can you divide it into parts or into functions? Can you make it fold up, knock down or portable? Can you combine functions? Can you add something to it? Can you make it disposable?

Perhaps you can make a change in the way it is energized. For example, can it be run by batteries instead of household electricity? Can it run with batteries instead of gasoline?

Can you improve the result that it produces? Can you speed it up or slow it down? Can you make it stretchable? Can you make it out of different material? Can you increase the number of functions it performs?

Can you change the state in which it is sold? For example, if it's sold as a powder, can you convert it to a liquid? Can you change the temperature at which it operates, is sold, or is shipped? Can you take an existing ready-built product and produce it in inexpensive kit form and provide simple, easy-to-build instructions that will make the final construction of the product fun for the prospective customer?

Some of the things that have evolved from this kind of thinking applied to existing products include small portable radios, cars of varying sizes, aluminum cans, plastic garbage cans, colored and scented facial tissues, multi-function pocket knives, campers, throw-away bottles, electric toothbrushes, electric knives, stretch socks, multi-head shavers, combination electronic entertainment centers, deodorant sticks, spray deodorant, frozen foods, stretch clothes, hi-fi kits, and food vending machines.

The preceding paragraphs provide a number of ideas for producing variations in existing products. The next question may be how do you analyze existing products for change possibilities. The simplest and quickest thing that any householder can do is refer to a Sears, Roebuck or some similar comprehensive product catalog. Scan it and try to develop thoughts about how you can vary products displayed in the catalog.

The hobbyist can readily come up with a number of ideas related to his hobby by scanning through hobby supply catalogs for the products that are commonly used in his field. You can pull a lot of ideas out of newspapers, books, encyclopedias, periodicals, and business catalogs such as the Thomas Register. An excellent place to start looking for ideas is your library.

Other sources of new product ideas are other people. Inventors are a significant source of new-product ideas, as well as the people that you come in contact with every day. You can obtain copies of new inventions from the U.S. Patent Office.

These new inventions are frequently reported in magazines such as *Popular Mechanics, Science and Mechanics,* and *Mechanics Illustrated.* In addition, you can scan the Official Gazette of the Patent Office in your public library for new patents. This publication is more comprehensive than the reporting that you'll find in the mechanics and new technology-type magazines. If you engage in this activity in an aggressive manner, you can subscribe to the gazette. The cost is about $20 a year. For further information, write to the U.S. Government Printing Office, Washington, D.C. 20402.

Another source of new products lies in government-owned patents and dedicated patents which may be used without payment of royalties or licensing fees. For further information on these patents, write to the United States Patent Office.

Now that we've explored the sources for new-product ideas and new-product patents, let's take a look at how you develop them for production. In the big manufacturing businesses in the country, the first step is the production of a working prototype. You can build your working prototype in your garage shop or you can have it built by a small shop that has appropriate facilities for the kind of construction that is involved. If the item is a relatively low-cost one, it's a good idea to have five or ten copies of the product made. These prototypes may then be used to validate the design and to effect improvements in it. They're also useful as selling samples. After the design has been frozen, you can develop the packaging, the marketing, and the whole plan with greater assurance of success.

HOW TO FIND SOURCES

One of the major keys to successful competitive manufacturing is the development of low-cost sources for raw materials, details, components, and subassemblies. As you get into these aspects of your manufacturing operation, you'll find that you can save as much as 1,000 percent in some cases by shopping around and exploring sources in considerable depth. Always get competitive bids or prices from several sources.

The logical place to begin your search for sources of raw materials, components, subassemblies, and assemblies is the classified section of the telephone directory. Search under the classifications that involve the kinds of materials and services that you are interested in. Then get on the telephone and make some visits to the more promising sources of supply. You'll also find sources of supply listed in periodicals that serve the product field that you are about to enter. Of course, the master-source of sources of supply is the Thomas Register. This is available in most public libraries and in the purchasing departments of companies of even relatively small size.

WHERE TO GET THE TALENT YOU NEED

Since you're a moonlighter and your manufacturing operation is a moonlight operation, it would seem logical that you'd get moonlighting employees. They can be obtained more reasonably than people who must earn a full-time living working for you, and they'll make concessions for future potential. Furthermore, this frees you from the fixed high-cost burden of keeping a staff of employees going on a full-time basis. You can usually arrange to hire moonlighters by the hour or on piecework as you need them; consequently, you have no established minimum expenses that you have to meet regardless of sales. You can make your costs of manufacture direct by using this method.

Don't overlook women as a source of workers. Just because men usually do the kind of work that you are thinking about, don't rule out the gals! More and more women are joining the work force; and in many precision industries such as electronics and precision mechanisms, women are starting to take over the assembly lines.

There's a tendency to under-place people in industry, that is, to hire people who are considerably better than the job they have to perform. Keep this in mind. Utilize people in jobs which match their abilities and challenge them rather than in jobs that are below their level of performance.

HOW TO GET PRODUCTION STARTED

In order to get your production started, you will have to obtain the machinery that is required to manufacture your product. Perhaps you'll need drills, saws, test instruments, and other equipment of this sort. These can sometimes be obtained on a lease basis. In many instances though, you'll be able to furnish all the tools you need from those that you may have in your backyard workshop.

Assuming that you do not have the tools, you might want to look into buying used equipment. If you'll check the classified ads, you may find bargains obtainable at considerably less cost than new tools and equipment. In a few instances, you'll find that you can buy used tools for less than the monthly lease price!

Of course you'll need raw materials, components, and possibly subassemblies. If you're in a large metropolitan area and have a stocking source with adequate warehouse facilities, you obviously don't have to do a great deal of stockpiling. However, materials in considerable demand may become scarce due to strikes at the factory, transportation strikes, or due to economic situations. You could be left holding the bag if you maintain too small an inventory.

At this point you have a product that is ready to sell. You have this product in a working, tested prototype form, and you've developed the drawings needed for contractor bidding and for manufacturing the product. In addition, you've made arrangements to purchase the raw materials, the components, and perhaps some of the details and subassemblies for the final assembly of the product from an array of sources. You've located the people that you need, a potential factory, and the needed tools and machines. Next, move your equipment into your building, get the utilities turned on, and get a sign up over the front door. Order a telephone and equip your office. Get organized for production by getting your supervision and workers in. Provide training where it's required. Then, start production.

HOW TO PRICE YOUR PRODUCT

The price of your product is based on the raw materials that go into it, the direct costs of labor required in its assembly, the indirect cost associated with the operation of the business (such as office expense, advertising, etc.), and the profit that you desire to make on your product.

Develop the cost of the raw materials that go into each copy of your product. Then develop the direct labor cost required in the assembly of the product and the handling of the materials. Once you have these, you have the direct cost. Next you take the total indirect cost of your operation for a year, and divide this cost by the number of products that you will manufacture per year. This gives you the indirect cost per unit of output and this is added into the other figures that you have developed. Finally, you add the profit that you desire to make. This gives you the total cost of a unit of your product.

MAKE OR BUY DECISIONS

Frequently you can buy a part for the manufacture of your product much less expensively than you can manufacture it yourself. If this is the case, there is no point in manufacturing the part yourself.

However, in many cases where a detail or a component can be bought elsewhere, it may be difficult to get the quality or some other feature in the product that you want, although the price might be competitive. In this case, you'll want to manufacture it for yourself. For example, General Radio, a major electronics instrument producer, to maintain quality makes many of the major components and subassemblies that go into its instruments.

Another factor that enters "make" or "buy" decisions hinges on proprietary information, ideas, and processes. Where you have a proprietary method or process, you might want to make the component or subassembly yourself in order to protect your process.

HOW TO MARKET YOUR PRODUCT

A product can be marketed in many, many ways. One of the naturals that you immediately think of for a home industry operation is to market the product by mail order. Direct mail-order sales to individuals is a business in itself, and there are not too many manufacturers who have gotten their start in this way. However, there are some who have done it successfully.

One of the best ways to get your product to market and to profit on your manufacturing capabilities is by selling your product to a wholesaler who sells retailers. The retailers make the individual sales.

The magic dream that many aspiring manufacturers have is to sell a large national retail organization, such as Sears, Roebuck, Western Auto, K-Mart, or one of the other large national chain-store retailers. It's always worth a try. You can approach these people and get orders for your product even before you start to manufacture it. Enter through the purchasing department. If you get a firm order, you may be able to use it as collateral to finance production.

The next best thing to try is to recruit a national sales force of independent salesmen through magazines such as *Specialty*

Salesman and *Salesman's Opportunity.* A number of my friends who are in relatively large mail-order operations tell me that they get better results on recruiting salesmen through the classified ads in these magazines than through the use of display space on a per-dollar advertising cost basis. *Popular Mechanics* and magazines of that nature may also be productive in recruiting salesmen for your product.

If you're going to recruit salesmen by mail, don't forget that you need literature that describes and helps to sell the product as well as literature that describes your proposition to the salesman.

Many a small manufacturing business got its start because the owner canvassed retail outlets in his hometown and got his product on the counter there. You'll usually find that dealers in your hometown have a special affinity for products manufactured there by small businesses and they'll usually give you a lot of help in launching the product if it's a good one.

In looking for outlets for your product, don't overlook the Yellow Pages in the telephone directory of your city and of other cities as a prospect source-list. Additional ideas on firms to contact can be found in trade directories of the various trade associations throughout the United States.

THE MAGIC OF PRODUCT SUCCESS

The magic of any product's success is coming up with a product that people want and can use that performs a useful function and costs less than competing products. But there are other tricks that provide additional magic for the sale of your product. And that is the matter of utilizing "kickers." For example, if your product can be merchandised for a profit through school, church, social, and other organizations, a large sales force is standing by. There are a number of candy companies that have built very successful businesses with this method.

If you can get a large organizational user to adopt your product, you'll add to its chances of success. For example, suppose you are manufacturing a chair. If you can win acceptance for your chair from a large organization such as Holiday Inns, you've got a pretty husky customer on your hands.

FORTUNES IN RE-MANUFACTURE

We've mentioned the business possibilities of re-manufacture and refurbishment earlier in the book. I can't emphasize enough the potential that exists in this type of business.

The reason that the potential in re-manufacture is so great is that the inflationary trend built into the American economy tends to drive the cost of everything that involves labor to continually higher levels. Consequently, a product manufactured a year ago cost less than a product manufactured today; and a product manufactured ten years ago, cost considerably less than that. Another factor that tends to make the cost of your re-manufacture raw materials a bargain is the fact that the user who is disposing of an item discounts the value tremendously. This is especially true if the unit is defective and requires repairs.

Re-manufacturing becomes a custom process unless you get into a high-volume area. Some of the high-volume areas include components for automobiles, air conditioners, and furniture. But even in these fields, there's a variation from product to product. The wise entrepreneur who can set up the required rehabilitation facilities, handle the stocking of repair parts, and manage the repair operations can make a killing in this field.

HOUSE MANUFACTURING FORTUNES

The manufacture of houses, the construction business, is one of the most profitable businesses in the United States. This business is profitable because there are plenty of detail corners in which additional profits can be made. Profits are made on the lot on which the house is built, as well as on the house itself.

The big "kicker" in the house manufacturing industry is the ease with which houses can be financed. Thus, the builder secures a construction loan when he begins construction of the house. This finances the building. When construction is completed and the house is sold to the owner, the owner secures financing through a mortgage loan. This may be a conventional loan or a government-insured FHA or VA loan.

Houses are generally manufactured on a subcontract basis. The builder is often merely a manager. Thus, he might use a foundation contractor to pour the foundation and to do the concrete work, a framing contractor to frame the house, a brick contractor to put up the walls, a roofing contractor, a plumbing contractor, an electrical contractor, and an air conditioning/heating contractor. At the outset he obtains plans for the house, either through a plan service which will generally make a set of plans available for $25 to $50 a set with a cost of perhaps $5 to $10 for each additional copy, or he may have a house designed to his own specifications. He solicits bids for the construction of the house, and obtains options on lots. Once he has obtained the bids and has secured options or has bought the lots, he goes to his bank and obtains financing for constructing the houses. Sometimes the banks will require that he have a mortgage loan commitment at the time he secures this interim financing.

When the builder has secured his interim loan, he commences construction on the property. Generally he will make arrangements to get his money from the bank as he needs it to pay off the subcontractors rather than taking a lump sum of money which will be idle during most of the construction process. At such time as he completes construction, he goes through the various inspections and arranges a closing on the property, at which time the property is sold, the mortgage is placed, and the buyer is on the note for the long-term payout of the property.

There are a number of things to remember in the home manufacturing business. First, on subcontracts, try to obtain three to five bids for each portion of the task. Try to obtain subcontracts which specify the period of time for performance, and if possible work penalty clauses into your subcontracts. The state of the economy may have something to do with the possibility of doing this. When construction people are in demand, it becomes very difficult to get any kind of penalty clause for a delay in performance. The time involved in the construction is an important cost item for the builder and it also affects his cash turnover and his pyramiding capabilities. Another consideration that the builder must keep in mind is the union situation in his area. Some builders utilize moonlighters on their jobs. Interior work that can be done early in the morning or late at night before or after the moonlighter leaves his regular job fits the bill best. In some towns there are existing situations that make this kind of operation impossible; but there are many places in the United States where this is practiced. Another factor that is important to the builder is the weather. Exterior construction in home manufacturing comes to an end during the winter months in some parts of the country. The astute builder in this geographical environment will try to have finished exteriors when the winter months come on so he can finish the interiors during this time.

CONSIDER THESE ASPECTS IN BUILDING

Another factor affecting the builder is the demand period on housing. Generally speaking, houses sell faster during the late spring, summer, and early fall months than during the remainder of the year. Occasionally there is a spurt in housing sales in January. The school situation appears to have considerable influence on the housing market.

There's an opportunity for vertical expansion in the housing business if the builder cares to develop the separate construction capabilities that are required in building a house and then uses these capabilities from within his organization instead of subcontracting them. The builder can further increase his profits by becoming, in addition, a developer.

The developer purchases a housing tract. He subdivides into lots and puts in improvements. (Occasionally he will buy an improved tract which has streets and utilities in.) The lots are subdivided and sold—some of them to other builders, who will in turn build houses on them and sell them—or the developer may reserve all of the lots for his own construction. If he does the latter, he develops a larger profit on each lot he sells. Through this process, he has a larger profit per lot in addition to the profit that he makes on each house he builds. Another advantage accrues from this type of operation: he can put up a field sales office and staff it. Yet another advantage is that all of the construction activity is centered at one location. Consequently, subcontractors can move in and work from house to house without too many transportation problems. This cuts transportation time, and permits him to move his crew to another house if a hold-up occurs on any of the others. This efficiency reduces costs and simplifies management.

Many fortunes have been made in house manufacture; this may possibly be your way to riches. I know a number of people who have gotten a start in the business by fixing up old houses after hours, doing the work themselves, and then reselling them. From this modest start several of these fellows have gone on to enter new-house manufacture, again working it on an after-hours basis and doing the construction themselves and with the help of some of their buddies. After building and selling a few houses on this basis, they went into the business full time.

OTHER MONEY-MAKING CONSTRUCTION VENTURES

There's plenty of money to be made in the construction business. In order to tap the market from a relatively small start, consider the building of garages, and other utility buildings that are not a part of the main structure. These buildings are generally very simple and easy to construct. They're not interesting to the larger building contractor because it isn't worth his management effort. Yet you can construct buildings of this type with just a few skilled craftsmen and some unskilled workers. A small ad under "Services" or "Building" in the classified section of your local newspaper will often put you in business.

Another construction venture which has business potential is house remodeling. Since these jobs are small, there aren't too many people interested in them. All in all, there is a market for construction jobs in the $500 to $5,000 range that is not adequately serviced. An imaginative person with a staff of moonlighting carpenters, electricians, and plumbers can readily tap these markets and make a substantial after-hours income. Bear in mind that most municipalities require a building permit for any modification to an existing building or the construction of an outbuilding.

I've mentioned the business of buying run-down houses and repairing them. This is another business that falls into the remanufacture category and one that can be very profitable. In order to make money at it, you've got to buy the properties at the right prices. Generally speaking, the more run-down they are, the less they can be bought for. However, be sure that there's a good foundation under the buildings you buy, that major electrical and plumbing repairs do not have to be made, and that the location of a building is such that it can be sold for a profit. The general rule of thumb is that the building, after it is fixed up, should not be the most expensive building in the neighborhood.

Additional opportunities in construction exist in the sale and erection of prefabricated buildings under franchise. These buildings are made from preassembled components and usually fall into the industrial and business categories. They're usually made of metal components, and variations in appearance are obtained by employing brick and other facades. These building franchises generally involve a relatively large business and investment, in contrast to the other construction businesses that we've talked about.

Another construction re-manufacturing business you might consider involves the mobile home. Used mobile homes can sometimes be purchased at bargain prices. These can be refurbished and repaired and sold at a profit.

HERE'S EXTRA HELP

These U.S. Government Printing Office publications will be helpful to you in establishing a manufacturing venture:

Developing and Selling New Products,
Gustav E. Larsen

Management Aids for Small Manufacturers,
SBA Annual No. 5

Starting and Managing A Small Building
Business, John R. Immer

The books cited above cost from about 50 cents to a dollar each. Check the latest U.S. Government Printing Office lists for exact prices.

Other publications which will be helpful include the Thomas Register (for sources of supply), textbooks in the manufacturing disciplines, and trade periodicals.

CHECKLIST FOR STARTING A MANUFACTURING BUSINESS

1. Find a product to manufacture.
2. Be sure that there's a demand for the product you select.
3. Design and develop the product. Freeze the design prior to production.
4. Develop sources of supply. Get competitive bids.
5. Build a talent and manpower pool to staff your factory.
6. Develop a sound financial program.

7. Find your factory and equip it.

8. Get production started.

9. Develop sound pricing. Don't overlook general overhead, pilferage, rejection, and other less obvious costs.

10. Develop a sound marketing scheme.

9

HOW TO MAKE A KILLING IN SERVICES

SERVICES ARE GROWING FAST!

The service industry is growing faster than manufacturing, mining, agriculture, construction, and the other facets of the activity that is ordinarily classified as "production." For example, in 1947, 36 billion hours were poured into manufacturing and mining activity. This number went up to only 38 billion man-hours in 1957. By 1967, it was 43 billion. Agricultural output dropped from 22 billion man-hours in 1947 to 9 billion in 1967. Construction went from 6 billion man-hours in 1947 to only 8 billion in 1967.

But look what happened to personal and professional services! In 1947, it stood at 18 billion man-hours. By 1957, it had grown to 22 billion! And, by 1967, it had grown to 27.4 billion man-hours! Note that the twenty-year growth here has been approximately 50 percent, whereas in manufacturing, the twenty-year growth was only about 20 percent. The growth in services that include finance, real estate, and insurance rose from 4 billion man-hours in 1947 to 7 billion man-hours in 1967, a growth rate of approximately 75 percent!

An article in the October, 1968, issue of *Fortune* magazine

161

entitled, "The Still-Bright Promise of Productivity," tells the story of the historic transition to a service society. The first sentence of the article reemphasizes the promise and opportunity of America. It points out that the increase in productivity in the United States in the last twenty years is equal to the entire annual production of the Soviet Union.

The prime essential in any service business is to render satisfactory service. The maintenance services that I had attempted to secure from others on my properties were by and large unsatisfactory. The interests of the serviceman (who apparently worked on a commission in most cases) always seemed to be to inflate the bill. Furthermore, on about half the service calls made, the work was not completed satisfactorily, and the company had to be called back for additional service. In almost every instance this was billed as an additional charge. In spite of telephone conversations and discussions with service company owners, it was impossible to secure any kind of adjustment. The attitude of the owners of these service companies seemed to be, "If you don't like our service try elsewhere—they'll charge you as much or more." This is a very negative business attitude and is the kind of thing that leads to the erection of competition.

> *Moonlight Fortune Tip (MFT) 32*
> Anytime a business starts to make exorbitant profits and to abuse its patrons, competition is sure to spring up.

That's a good thought to put at the top of your list of "how to succeed in business."

DEVICE MAINTENANCE AND REPAIR SERVICES

There are a large number of services that are required in the maintenance and repair of an automobile. These include general automobile repair, top and body repair, battery and ignition service, radiator repair, tire repair, auto paint and body shops, auto glass shops, brake repair shops, wheel-axle and spring shops, automobile parking lots, auto and truck rentals, and others.

A large number of miscellaneous repair services are listed in Department of Commerce publications. These include: electrical repair shops, radio and TV repair shops, refrigerator service and repair, watch, clock, and jewelry repair, reupholstery and furniture repair, armature rewinding shops, gunsmith shops, locksmith shops, musical instrument repair shops, lawn mower, saw, knife, and tool sharpening shops, welding shops, typewriter repair shops, and numerous others.

Repair shops generally have a flat rate for a service call which includes the first 15 or 30 minutes of effort. Additional time is generally charged by the hour. Rates range from $7 to $20 an hour (to the customer) for most services in most parts of the USA. A flat charge ranging from $4 to $10 is usually collected for devices brought to the shop which require 30 minutes or less to repair. Most service operators charge two to five times the hourly rate they pay the serviceman. This is not as unreasonable as it may sound since they don't sell every hour of a man's time. Some service-company owners put their servicemen on commission and pay them 30 to 50 percent of the labor charges plus a percentage on parts. This will give you some ideas on establishing rates for the services you sell.

GETTING YOURS IN THE $150 BILLION LEISURE AND TRAVEL MARKET

In 1968, Merrill Lynch, Pierce, Fenner and Smith published "The Billion-Dollar Leisure Market." In this publication, Merrill Lynch noted the growing leisure time of the American people and the growing expenditure in this market. This was not particularly new to me since I was familiar with studies made by Stanford Research Institute and the Arthur D. Little Co.

Here are some of the services that figure into the big travel and recreation market: dance halls, dance studios, entertainment bureaus, dance orchestras, entertainers, bowling, billiards and pool, commercial sports such as baseball and football clubs, promotion of these, ownership in teams, management of individual sports contestants, race-track operations, including racing stables, automobile racing and dog racing, golf courses, golf clubs, swimming pools, skating rinks, canoe and boat rentals, amusement parks, amusement concessions at amusement parks, motion-picture theaters, coin-operated amusement devices, hobby halls, and others.

The travel market constitutes a large portion of the leisure market. It seems that in order to be anybody, you must have travelled. While a trip around the United States used to seem exciting to the secretary in Pittsburgh who had never been anywhere, she now looks forward to Puerto Rico, Mexico, Japan, or Europe.

So how do you get yours in the $150 billion travel and leisure market? Plenty of people have made money with travel agencies over the years. Transportation companies themselves like Braniff International or American Airlines have benefited from the travel mania that has beset the United States. All of these companies are potential customers for any business you'll develop that will help them increase profitability or cut costs.

Another aspect of the leisure market worth exploring includes motels, convention centers, restaurants, and the associated concessions.

But that isn't all—there's more! The arrangers—the people who arrange the trips, the people who arrange for conventions—they've also got something going for them.

One of the biggest gold mines in the United States today is the restaurant and hot-food business. This business has grown from the around-the-corner family restaurant or delicatessen into a lacework of franchises ranging from fried chicken to enchilada sandwiches. There are thousands of these franchises spread from coast to coast and border to border. At the present time one wonders how so many of them can succeed in some of the saturated locations that they occupy. It is probable that some of these franchises will fail.

RESTAURANTS MAKE GOOD MONEY

One of my successful restaurant operator friends has had his place for approximately 12 years. He got into the business because he built the building and afterwards couldn't rent it. He indicates that his restaurant makes approximately $30,000 a year for him. For this, he works about 12 hours a day, 6 days a week. One not too apparent advantage that he does enjoy which makes his $30,000 income bigger after taxes than an equivalent income is that he owns the building and therefore enjoys some tax shelter on the amortization. He's got something else going for him: The property on which his restaurant is located is increasing in value very rapidly. It is probable that by the time he has the property completely paid out, he will be able to sell it for more than 10 times what it cost him. I own a restaurant, myself, and value it as one of my best investments.

If you want to get into the restaurant business, I recommend that you obtain a book called "Starting and Managing a Small Restaurant" published by the Small Business Administration and available through the U.S. Government Printing Office, Washington, D.C. 20402. This book is one of many in the starting and managing series published by the Small Business Administration. In it, you learn of some of the problems that restaurant operators encounter, the different kinds of restaurants that you might start, franchise operations, some of the nuts and bolts of running a restaurant, some thoughts on your suitability for this kind of business, and some of the financial requirements. This book takes you through the process of launching the restaurant, taking the first steps, finding the location, organizing, and preparing for your opening.

Some of the problems that beset the small restaurant operator include these:

1. Today's diners expect first-rate eating facilities. Consequently, furnishings are expensive.

2. Commercial food equipment is costly. Although you might start with ordinary kitchen equipment, the size of your operation would be severely limited.

3. Labor costs are high. If you and your wife operate a restaurant and employ just one other person to wash the dishes and clean up, you'll need sales of approximately $3,000 to $3,500 a month in order to meet expenses and the salary of your wife and yourself.

4. The profits are modest. The profits from food alone are small. The net profit of restauranteurs before income taxes on a national average is less than 5 percent of total sales. Net profits of 10 percent of sales is considered a high profit. Generally speaking, a restaurant must do $50,000 a year or more in business in order to be profitable.

5. Turnover is limited. Seat turnover is limited because most of your customers tend to come during short eating periods in the day. Hence, if you have a seating capacity of 50, it is probable that you will be limited to 150 customers during the lunch hour.

THE HOBBY MARKET

The leisure market encompasses more than the travel, shelter, and restaurant markets. It includes the fabulous hobby market. One company that has successfully tapped the hobby market is the Heath Company. The Heath Company was started a number of years ago in the airplane-kit market and then switched over to electronic kits in the late '40's. Heath Company sold electronic kits which utilized surplus parts. Volume soon made the surplus market an inadequate source. The company is now a leader in hi-fi, electronic service, and hobby kits.

Norm Edmund is a successful penetrator of the hobby market. Norm started by selling surplus optical goods to hobbyists and then branched into the full scientific hobby field.

One of the greatest leisure industries of all is the education industry. A number of educators have stated the greatest aim of education is to provide productive pursuits for leisure time. Some of the companies that have tapped this market are The Dale Carnegie Institute, Arnold Palmer activities, and similar "how-to-enjoy-your-sport" enterprises. The Famous Artists and the Famous Writers operations are similar educational activities that have benefited from the proliferating leisure market.

PROVIDE PROFESSIONAL SERVICES AND REAP A FORTUNE

One of the hottest areas in the services field is professional services. Doctors, lawyers, dentists, accountants, and consulting organizations earn big fees. Scientific laboratories which provide services to the professional fraternity have earned good incomes over the years, too. Needless to say, an investment in the long education required for the practice of medicine and one of the associated specialties or dentistry will pay off in high income during the professional's life. Law practice follows close behind, although the young lawyer generally has a more difficult time getting started than the doctor does. The proliferating snare of laws and legal requirements and the increasing record keeping that has been brought about by our modern government and our rapidly growing society have made it a little less difficult to get started in the legal field. Accountants, too, are benefiting from the increasing complexity and prosperity that the United States is enjoying. Anyone with an accounting background can very easily go into a part-time accounting practice and acquire enough bookkeeping and income-tax jobs to earn $5,000 to

$10,000 a year in his spare time. If he's a hard worker, he can even top the $10,000 figure with his spare-time work. An accountant working full time with just one bookkeeping assistant can, after he has gotten his Certified Public Accountant rating, earn $20,000 to $40,000 a year.

Engineers also rank in the top professional services and make excellent showings when it comes to earning money. They earn $9,000 to $30,000 working for large companies, and frequentlv $5,000 to $15,000 a year from moonlight engineering work.

Although a moonlight income of $5,000 to $15,000 a year may not sound like a real fortune, just think what it will grow to if invested in property, stocks, other small businesses, or even tax-free bonds!

PERSONAL SERVICES THAT DO AND DON'T MAKE FORTUNES

There's a broad array of personal services that are purchased by individuals. These services include the following: laundries, dry cleaning, beauty and barber shops, motion pictures, pet salons, linen supplies, diaper services, dry cleaning plants, photo studios, shoe repair, funeral service, clothing alterations, fur repair and storage, turkish baths, massage salons, reducing salons, costume and dress suit rental agencies, rug and furniture cleaning establishments, coin-operated service machine establishments, check-room concessions, and numerous other minor services.

Some of these services are highly profitable; others are, generally speaking, marginal money-makers. To be successful in any of these personal service businesses, it is essential that you establish volume, that you build a reputation for your service, and that the operation be tightly managed. This is sometimes difficult to do as an absentee owner. However, you can form a joint venture with a person who has skill in one of the personal service disciplines but who lacks the financing and the management savvy to run the business. In order for this kind of venture to be successful, the partner that you choose must, in addition to being competent in his own specialty field, respect your capability as a management consultant and as a partner. He must respect the contribution that your investment is making toward his getting started. One of my friends who is a partner in a number of beauty salons, earns approximately $1,000 a month from these ventures. His original investment was approximately $5,000.

SPECIAL SERVICES TO BUSINESS MAKE BIG PROFITS

Businesses require special services which they often purchase. They do so because the capital investment required or a full-time employee to perform a required service isn't justified. Hence, businesses know the value of business services and are willing to pay well for them.

Here are some of the business services that are productive money-makers: advertising, credit bureaus, collection agencies, duplicating, mailing lists, stenographic services, blueprinting, photocopying, news syndicates, employment agencies, research and development laboratories, testing laboratories, business-management consulting services, detective agencies, protective services, interior decorating, sign-painting shops, auctioneers, auction houses, coin-operated machine rentals, photo finishing laboratories, telephone answering services, window display services, trading stamps, water-softening services, and others.

UTILITY AND TRANSPORTATION CONCEPTS PAY OFF BIG

Now let's stretch our thinking for just a moment. Some of the most successful businesses in the United States are utility businesses: These businesses furnish energy and communication services at the present time. Recently we've heard a lot of talk about computer utilities. There's also been a lot of talk about the postal service becoming a private utility operated by a nonprofit organization or by a big corporation. So you're not too far out of line if you think in terms of establishing your own utility. One of the looming problems on the horizon is the United States transportation crisis. Automobiles are proliferating, a large portion of our real estate is dedicated to highways, and the overall crowding is causing almost unbearable delays. The cost of transportation is constantly increasing, and the pollutants generated by the large number of internal combustion engines on the highways are fouling our atmosphere to a dangerous level. Consequently, the transportation utilities (railroads, airlines, bus companies, and taxi operators) are in for major change. The U.S. Department of Transportation is conducting research and development activity as well as innovative demonstration experiments with existing equipment that will lead to many new concepts in transportation. Many of tomorrow's millionaires will have made their fortunes by jumping on the transportation bandwagon today.

In Dallas, Texas, Sam Wyly started University Computing. He is one of the pioneers in developing what is known as a "computer utility." The concept is this: His company owns or leases a large number of computers at strategic locations throughout the world. Subscribers to his utility can use these computers on a scheduled and on a demand basis for a fee. Thus, a company that does not require a given computer on a full-time basis has to pay only for the computer time that it uses. Furthermore, the computer workload of most companies is almost ideally suited to a number of computers rather than to one computer. Hence, a computer-utility customer has available to him a large number of computers, each specifically designed for a special kind of job.

Another utility that is showing considerable future promise is the TV cable industry. It began as CATV (Community Antenna TV) and has considerable promise for broader applications.

Most moonlighters in utilities start with a small operation such as the formation or acquisition of a taxi company, a small rural telephone company, a local bus service, or a CATV franchise. The investment usually ranges around $10,000 cash with

$50,000 to $200,000 in debt. The high leverage is possible because the property serves as collateral.

A FRANCHISE CAN GIVE YOU A HEAD START

Franchising has developed into a major United States business. Franchising operates in this way: A company develops a product or a service, goes into the business and succeeds at it. At that point, the company has the choice of growing within itself or expanding by franchising others to engage in the same business in other locations in the United States and throughout the world. Franchising has become a favorite way to go because it enables the company to expand, and automatically provides distribution and financing.

The franchisor usually charges fees and gets a percentage of the action of the franchisee. At the present time, there are close to half a million United States franchise holders. They sell everything from food to services, and engage in equipment rentals. Franchise holders grossed more than $60 billion in 1967.

Coca-Cola is the acknowledged initiator of franchising in American industry. It began its franchising activity by licensing its bottling plants. The automobile business and the associated gasoline business was another form of franchising that developed long ago. A & W Root Beer Company is another early franchisor. They began in 1922 and now have over 2,000 franchises nationally.

Franchising as it is known today began in 1935 when Howard Johnson licensed a restaurant in Orleans, Massachusetts. The operation was successful, and today there are over 800 Howard Johnson restaurants across the United States and more than 350 motor lodges (the first one opened in 1954) that bear the Howard Johnson name.

There are approximately 800 national franchisors. It is estimated that better than 20 percent of the nation's independent enterprises are franchises. In 1967, some 25,000 individuals secured franchises.

Big business is entering the franchising area. General Foods, for example, acquired Burger Chef, and Pillsbury owns the Burger King chain. The trend is emphasized by the Wall Street reaction. For example, Minnie Pearl came out in May of 1968 at 20, and by the end of the first day, it had moved up to 40, and the next few days it moved up to 50 points.

The variety of businesses available in the franchise field is staggering. For example, General Spray Service of Katonah, New York, puts out franchises on an automated process for seeding and treating lawns and gardens. The franchisee pays $3,850 for a truck, patented spraying device, and complete training. The company expects each franchise holder to earn at least $300 a week over a 30-week season. Another franchise is the discotheque Arthur. This is the creation of Sybil Christopher, the former wife of actor Richard Burton. An Arthur franchise calls for a minimum investment of $100,000, which includes a $25,000 licensing fee, and $25,000 to $50,000 to set up the club plus operating capital.

The power of the franchise lies in the fact that it removes some of the pitfalls of starting the small business. It provides some of the entrepreneurial knowledge that is essential to operating. Unfortunately, the franchisee usually has to pay a high price in any franchise operation. The franchising business is also beset by fraud operations that exploit the attractiveness of a business by selling franchises to people who do not have the confidence to ultimately succeed or that sell ideas not fully developed nor fully proven. Frankly, a rigorous study of a number of books such as the one you are now reading, some discussions with businessmen, your Chamber of Commerce people and with others who are striving to set up their own businesses can provide much of the business savvy that a franchisor can offer, at considerably less cost.

The U.S. Department of Commerce's Business and Defense Services Administration published "Franchise Company Data" in February, 1968. This publication lists approximately 100 franchise operations and provides a considerable amount of background information and answers to questions which the prospective franchisee should study before entering any kind of franchise. The franchise businesses listed in this publication require capital ranging from as little as $300 to more than $100,000 to get started. The majority of the companies listed require as a minimum less than $25,000. You can obtain copies of this book at your local U.S. Department of Commerce Field Office, or from the U.S. Government Printing Office.

HOW TO START YOUR OWN SERVICE BUSINESS

Before you decide to get into any service business, make an assessment of the market in the locality where the operation is to occur. You can make this survey by checking the telephone directory to see how many people are already in the business in your city. Your local Chamber of Commerce can also furnish information about businesses of the type that you are interested in entering. Then on the basis of the population and on the basis of the distribution of these services within your community determine how many potential customers are available to each of these businesses. It's a good idea to take a map and pinpoint the locations. Now it's true that location is not too critical for some service businesses such as those where the service orders are taken over the telephone. However, if you're considering personal services where the customer brings the work into the shop, it becomes essential that you choose a location that is strategically located.

The Small Business Administration and the Department of Commerce publish information on most service businesses. You'll do well to investigate statistics that they've accumulated.

Most of these statistics are gathered in the Statistical Abstract of the United States which is published every year by the U.S. Department of Commerce. This book is available through the U.S. Government Printing Office and it costs approximately $5 in the hard cover edition. For your $5 you'll get over a thousand pages of statistics of every kind imaginable. This book is, in my estimation, a real "must" for any big-time, moonlight moneymaker.

In conducting your market survey of the service businesses in your locality that are in competition with the business that you propose to start, you'll want to talk to some of your friends and see how they feel about the available services. If you detect a large measure of dissatisfaction with the available service, it's an indication that there's room for you. However, there's something else to be on the lookout for: it may be very difficult to perform satisfactory service in the selected business due to labor, training, or some other special problem. If you can detect and pinpoint special problem areas, address yourself to solving them before you try to enter the business.

Assuming that you determine that there is a definite need for the service business that you have selected, and that the possibility of its succeeding is great, the next step is to start action to get your business established. If you have done your homework by researching this service field in your local library and by obtaining any publications which the Department of Commerce has available (see last section in this chapter), you're ready to proceed. The steps that you'll take in getting the business started follow closely those outlined in some of the previous discussions in this book.

HOW TO ESTABLISH PRICES AND RATES

Establish prices and rates for your services in a businesslike manner. Compute your direct labor cost and the cost of materials. This is your direct cost. Then determine your indirect overhead which includes all other expenses. Compute the cost of each hour of service that you'll perform on this basis. Then, to arrive at the cost which you'll bill the customer, double the number that you come up with, and add a percentage for time that you won't be able to sell. This contingency allowance should be about 20 percent. (You'll already have some contingency as a result of the doubling process.) Keep the ranges cited earlier in this chapter in mind as a check. An average range of $8 to $12 an hour to the customer is probably realistic for most skilled services in most of the USA for 1969 with a 3 to 5 percent increase for each successive year.

10 LOW-COST BOOKS TO HELP YOU START

The "Starting and Managing Series" published by SBA includes books on 10 specific service businesses that you should study if you are going to enter any kind of service business. Even if none of these books discusses the specific business you want to enter, they can help you develop a good feel for the service business in general. The numbers below indicate the volume number in the "Starting and Managing Series." I'm listing the subject-matter part of the title only; prefix with "Starting and Managing a Small _____." Most of them cost less than 50 cents each.

2. Credit Bureau and Collection Service
3. Service Station
4. Bookkeeping Service
6. Aviation Fixed Base Operation
7. Motel
8. Duplicating and Mailing Service
9. Restaurant
12. Dry Cleaning Business
14. Carwash
16. Shoe Service Shop

10

LEASE, RENT, SELL AND "CREATE" YOUR WAY TO UNTOLD WEALTH

RENTALS PROVIDE INCOME CONTINUALLY

One of the beauties of the rental business is that you never give up your product and you collect continual income from it. But there are more advantages, which is the subject of this chapter. When you sell a product, you make a profit on it, once and finally. You will never again make a profit on that same product except by servicing it during its lifetime or by providing expendable refills for it. Rental property, on the other hand, earns a continual income.

New innovations and applications of the rental concept make the term "rental property" incomplete. For example, the rental and leasing of equipment and people (actually their labor) has become big business as typified by Kelly Girls, etc. Frequently the rental of a piece of property includes human services such as those provided with a computer. In any event, rental business is based on time, and you retain ownership in the property. The "people" rental agencies own the people in the sense that they call them as needed, pay them for actual work performed, and then collect "rent" for the use of the people.

SIX BASIC CHARACTERISTICS OF A MONEY-MAKING RENTAL

Any property or product *must possess one or more* of these six characteristics to make it a profitable rental item:

1. High cost;
2. Low-usage, infrequently used;
3. Possess utility;
4. A broad demand for its use;
5. Indispensable, special utility;
6. Labor-saving or a money-making capability or advantage.

Any product or property must have one or more of these six characteristics in order to make people rent it. Now let's take a look at each of them.

If the cost of a product is high, a large segment of the population will not be able to afford to buy it. Consequently, these people will rent the product or the property. The most frequent example and biggest business of all is rental real estate including residential, industrial, and business properties.

Another feature which tends to make an object or a device rentable is a low-usage feature. Typical examples are floor buffers, house jacks, trailers, trailer hitches, and as far as an individual is concerned, a pickup truck. Since the individual does not use these items frequently, he would rather rent than buy them.

Utility is another feature that any rentable product must possess. For example, antiques and works of art have limited utility. Consequently, they are not fast-moving rental items (in spite of this, there are some people who are making profits in renting paintings!).

Broad demand, that is, an occasional demand for the product by a large number of people is essential for you to get a high percentage of rental time on anything that you are going to rent.

Hence, a large electric drill is in occasional demand by a large number of people.

Indispensable, special utility is another feature that tends to make for a good rental situation. Typical example here is sickroom equipment. A requirement for a wheelchair on a temporary basis is one example of this kind of thing. Yet, very few families would want to have a wheelchair around the house when it wasn't required.

Labor-saving and money-making utility and capability are additional characteristics that tend to make an item profitable as a rental unit. Hence, trucks are frequently leased and rented to businesses because these trucks can produce income. Rented equipment is expensed 100 percent for income-tax purposes, whereas owned equipment is depreciated over a period of years.

REAL ESTATE RENTAL ZOOMS NET WORTH

Many of America's millionaires got their starts through real estate rental. We've already discussed the ways in which leverage can be used to buy properties for a small percentage of their total value. Consequently, it doesn't cost a lot of money to get into the rental business. Another feature of rental real estate is that because of its high dollar value and long-term finance features, its depreciation provides tax-shelter advantages. The demand for property is great. People require a place to live.

Since rental properties provide a spendable income, and an additional income in the form of equity in the property, they tend to make the investor's net worth increase. But the investor has a number of other things working for him that makes his net worth grow even more rapidly. These things are appreciation due to the location of the property, appreciation due to inflation (a large percentage of a building is labor), and appreciation due to the scarcity of land. Hence, the real estate investor's net worth zooms!

AUTOMOTIVE AND EQUIPMENT RENTALS

The car and equipment rental businesses have grown at a staggering rate in the United States over the past two decades. These businesses account for large incomes, and at the present time, there are about 10 or 20 car rental companies which work through franchises, plus a large number of independent operators. There are about five large rent-all franchisors and many specialized equipment rental franchisors. All of these businesses are prospering and enjoying a very lucrative business. The franchisees sometimes face a rough start, but after two or three years, most of them do well.

There are a number of ways that you can get into the car or equipment rental business. One of the easiest ways is through a franchise. Here are some companies that franchise dealers in the United States:

Auto/Trailer Rentals
Airways Rent-A-Car Systems
Avis
Budget Rent-A-Car
Dollar-A-Day Rent-A-Car
Econo-Car International
Hertz
Move Truck Rental Systems
National
Willard Leasing

Equipment Rentals
A to Z Rentals
Abbey Rents
Liberty Leasing
United Rent-All

Of course you don't have to obtain a franchise to get into the rental business. You've got the assets to get into the business if you have a small garage workshop. You can get started by renting the tools that you now own. One of the problems that you'll encounter is that there'll be demands for things that you don't have. It's a very simple matter to augment the tools and equipment that you now have with others and hence get off to a better start in the business. Since you can finance everything that you use in your rental business, you don't have to invest the full equipment price. Through the use of the leverage techniques that were discussed earlier in this book, it's possible for you to get additional equipment for 5 to 20 percent of the total cost down. Your rentals then will take care of servicing your debt and throw off a profit.

One of the features of the car rental business is that the sale of the car after a year of use is a part of the operation. Since cars in rental fleets are maintained at a high level, they are generally in cream-puff condition when they're sold off, and consequently demand highest prices. Most of the larger car-rental operators wholesale their cars. However, there's an additional opportunity for profit for the small rental fleet operator in retailing his cars. Not all automobile rentals are on a day-to-day basis. Some companies in the automobile leasing business lease cars for a month, a year, or several years. Again, the resale of the car is a part of the overall profit picture.

LEARN FREE FROM THE FRANCHISORS

You can learn quite a bit about launching any kind of business from franchise operations. I cited BDSA's "Franchise Company Data For Equal Opportunity In Business" (available from U.S. Government Printing Office) in the previous chapter. Get a copy and study it. It will give you some idea of the capital requirements and other pertinent factors for specific businesses. Then visit franchise operations in the specific area of business that's of interest to you. See how they display, price, stock, and bill their products. Talk to the franchisee and get his opinion of the operation. Write to the franchisor and get his information. You can rest assured that it will be a pretty hard sell, particularly if you have a substantial financial status. Whether you decide to become a franchisee or operate as an independent, you'll learn quite a bit from your inquiries.

> *Moonlight Fortune Tip (MFT) 33*
> Use your right of inquiry to the hilt. Ask
> questions; send for information; study modes
> of operation.

PROFITABLE WHOLESALING

The distributor, jobber, and wholesaler are basic links in getting the product to the retailer who ultimately sells the consumer. The terms "distributor," "jobber," and "wholesaler" are sometimes used interchangeably. The term "distributor" is generally used in connection with a wholesaler who carries a complete line of one or more manufacturers. The term "jobber" generally refers to a wholesaler who buys odd lots of merchandise as a major part of his business.

As a wholesaler, you'll generally warehouse for the retailer, although you may have large orders "drop shipped" to retailers. Your buying must be geared to the market or you'll end up with shelves of slow moving merchandise. This ties up your capital and limits your turnover. To make out in wholesaling, put the 10 principles of Chapter 4 to work for you.

Wholesalers generally work through 30-day open accounts. With the monthly statement date and return time, this can stretch the payout on merchandise purchased one day after the statement date to 45 days. Most wholesalers give a discount for payment in 10 days; some give a discount for paying within 10 or 15 days of statement date. If you can keep your sales dealings in cash or work most of your accounts in 10 days, you'll reduce your capital requirements.

You can start a wholesale business from your home. Use your garage or basement for warehousing. Try to deal in something which puts specialized knowledge to work. Use Chamber of Commerce lists and the Yellow Pages of the Telephone Directory to develop mailing and prospects lists. Use Thomas Register and the Yellow Pages (Manufacturers) to develop sources of supply.

> *Moonlight Fortune Tip (MFT) 34*
> Wholesaling is a logical moonlight business
> that can provide a big payoff.

PROFITABLE RETAILING

Large fortunes have been made in retailing. The field is wide open to the innovative entrepreneur who can find a different approach to retailing. I don't believe that the "Mom and Pop" store is the kind of business that you're interested in getting into. The "Mom and Pop" store was characterized by no salary, with the profits serving to compensate for the time that the proprietors put into it. Of course, there are exceptions. There are "Mom and Pop" stores that eventually grew up into large businesses. But in this day and time, this is hardly the optimum formula.

If you want to build a great business, it's a good idea to study great businesses. I recommend a book called *The Great Merchants;*[1] it covers retailing from the Hudson Bay Company to the present day. Included are accounts of such businesses as Brooks Brothers, Tiffany's, Filene's, Marshall Field, Brentano's, Macy's, A & P, F. W. Woolworth Co., Sears, Roebuck & Co., Lane Bryant, J. C. Penney Co., Neiman-Marcus, Ohrbach's, Korvette, and others. The studies include the growth history and some of the gimmicks that these companies used in approaching their market.

---

[1] Tom Mahoney and Leonard Sloan, *The Great Merchants* (rev. ed.; New York: Harper & Row, Publishers, Inc., 1966).

The specialty shop provides the easiest and lowest investment route to take in retailing. Specializing permits you to concentrate your energies and your capital. Your wife may wish to operate it as Emma K., the wife of a prosperous builder, does in my hometown.

If you're really ambitious, you might wish to combine a wholesale and a retail operation. To do it effectively, sell retail up front, and wholesale only from the back to known retailers and dealers.

These low-cost SBA publications, available from the U.S. Government Printing Office, may prove helpful:

Starting and Managing a Small Business of Your Own (Volume 1)

Starting and Managing a Small Retail Hardware Store (Volume 10)

Starting and Managing a Small Retail Drugstore (Volume 11)

Starting and Managing a Swap Shop or Consignment Shop (Volume 15)

You can have a chain of retail stores without clerk overheads by getting into the automatic vending business. Get SBA's *Starting and Managing a Small Automatic Vending Business* (Volume 13) to study the field. One of my friends places coin-operated laundry equipment in apartments. He takes in about $75 a month for each two-washer–one-dryer set. His investment is about $700 per set. The equipment pays out in less than a year! It's a good moonlight business.

YOU CAN MAKE A MILLION WITH WORDS

You can make a million dollars with your words. The only salesman that a mail-order house has is its catalog—a collection of words and pictures. If the catalog says the right words, the house prospers and grows rapidly. There are thousands of them operating in the USA to prove it.

You can double or even quadruple your business every year through your words—your advertising and sales approaches. Whether you're moonlighting as a retailer, a wholesaler, a manufacturer, a real estate or insurance agent, a car dealer, or what have you, **you can make a million dollars faster with the right words.**

Your approach to selling and advertising is important. Your sales pitches and ads must have the right appeals, say the right things, and contain the right words. Furthermore, your ads must appear in the right publication, the appropriate section of the publication, and must stand apart from the ads around them. Similarly, your sales presentations must be made to the right people—the people who are authorized to buy!

Make your ad or "pitch" fit the purpose. If you have a product that is commonly used by women, address your presentation to women. If you want men to buy the product as a gift for women, address the pitch to men. If you're trying to recruit engineers, start an ad off with "WANTED: ENGINEERS" or just "ENGI-NEERS." The point is, **appeal to the right audience for your product!**

THREE SUBTLE PROFIT FACTS

There are profit-making ventures that you can launch without a single penny. We've talked about some of the possibilities in earlier chapters. The major factors in these "no cash" ventures were the provision of a service, exercise of the mind's creativity, and the application of technical knowledge. This section probes the details of the latter two factors and the new dimensions of the future. The subtle profit facts that this section will help you exploit are:

1. Your mind is a bottomless resource of creative output that **can be converted** directly to cash.

2. The past provides guides for the future which your mind can convert into profit-taking vision.

3. Any technological advance induces a series of momentous changes loaded with profit opportunities.

Your mind is the source of inventions, innovations, new techniques, business ideas, and seeds for creation. The creation may take the form of a book, advertising copy, a painting, a sculpture, or a creative service. You may develop the idea for forming and financing a new company, exploiting an invention, providing a new service, or you may create a new invention. In doing any of these things, you're extracting cash from your mind. The government recognized the cash value of these mental products by implementing a system of patents, copyrights and trademarks.

The future will not be a carbon copy of the past. But the past contains a pattern of trends, which, combined with present knowledge, enables you to extrapolate the future. You learn to do this just a little better during each succeeding year of your life. As you develop your vision for the future, you develop your profit potential. Early investors in the telephone and the Ford automobile profited handsomely. Today's investor in the future of the computer, pollution controls, medical technology, and automation will profit handsomely in the years ahead.

Any technological advance induces great changes that create numerous new industries. Just as the automobile created the new highway, repair, service, fuel, tire, and auto parts industries yesterday, so will the computer create new services, new ways of doing things, and new businesses in the future.

These three conclusions are the key to great riches, wealth, and power. Their validity has been proven again and again by men who have been in the mainstream of American progress. We're going to put them on our list of Moonlight Fortune Tips to burn them into our fortune building thoughts.

Moonlight Fortune Tip (MFT) 35
Your mind is a bottomless resource of creative output that can be converted directly to cash.

Moonlight Fortune Tip (MFT) 36
The past provides guides for the future which your mind can convert into profit-taking vision.

Moonlight Fortune Tip (MFT) 37
Any technological advance induces a series of momentous changes loaded with profit opportunities.

HOW TO PROFIT ON CHANGE

You can profit on change by being alert to changes and exploiting them quickly. Changes occur in every facet of our lives every day. Be alert especially to these changes which provide substantial new opportunities:

1. Technological
2. Economic
3. Social
4. Industrial and Business

Technological changes occur as the result of new technology, applications, and inventions. You need not possess technical competence in the new field to profit on it, but technical expertise will increase the avenues to profit that you can tap. These are the red-hot fields which are on the brink or already in the process of explosive growth:

1. Computers and Computer Technology
2. Automation and Controls
3. Pollution Controls
4. Construction Technology
5. Medical Technology
6. Education and Education Technology

7. Waste Disposal and Salvage

8. Service Technology

You'll note that all of these fields are prodded by one or more of the three other areas of change—economic, social, industrial and business—cited earlier. The old idea of technological progress was centered around the lone inventor or innovator in his laboratory or workshop. During recent decades emphasis shifted to the research laboratory. In the latter part of the last decade, there were some soul-searching reassessments of the results. Many corporate managers are beginning to view research laboratories and research activities as a luxury.

The major factor which is causing big business to take a look at its research activities is that sizeable laboratory expenditures may result in as small a yield as one product per 1,000 projects. The November 15, 1968, issue of *Forbe's* magazine indicated that 1968 R & D expenditures by industry approached only $9 billion. Eugene N. Beesley of Eli Lilly and Company, stated: "The bloom is coming off the rose. There are many companies who view the results of R & D over the past twenty years with some disappointment."

Some 10,000 new technical products are developed each year, and of these, approximately 2,000 new products survive in the market. This is a pretty low yield when one considers that there are some 15,000 industrial research laboratories in the United States. Nevertheless, there's plenty of opportunity left for the moonlight entrepreneur.

HOW TO GET THE BIG IDEAS THAT MAKE FORTUNES

Countless fortunes have been made with ideas that didn't exploit change or pertain to invention. Ideas that improve the status quo in any field can be profitable. They're generally based on the recognition of a need and its satisfaction. These are the usual steps in the process that leads to money-making ideas.

1. *Recognition of a Need.* You discover resource waste (manpower, material, money, etc.), inconvenience, or frustration in an activity.

2. *Development of a Remedy or Circumvention.* You develop a method, technique, device, or scheme for remedying or circumventing the need causation. *This is the new idea.*

3. *Adoption Marketing.* You develop a way to profit on the adoption of your idea. This is the key that many would-be idea men never develop. If you change the world without personal profit, you can be a great (but poor) philanthropist. If you change a minute facet of the world and profit in the process, you're a great (and rich) entrepreneur.

Here are some outside helps for increasing your money-making ideation:

Your Creative Power, Alex Osborn,
Charles Scribner's Sons, New York, 1948.
(Also in paperback—Dell Publishing Co., Inc.)

The Art of Clear Thinking, Rudolph Flesch,
Harper & Row, Publishers, Inc., New York, 1951.
(Also in Collier Books paperback.)

Discover Needs and Fill Them, Forrest H. Frantz, Sr.
Aim & Step Associates, Garland, Texas, 1964.
(LP phono record and printed guide.)

Smart Money Shortcuts to Becoming Rich,
Tyler Hicks, Parker Publishing Co.,
West Nyack, N.Y., 1966.

DOLLARS FOR CREATIVITY—NO INVESTMENT NEEDED

There are numerous paths to riches that require no investment whatsoever. Most of these paths to riches start in the mind and use the mind—and your other personal resources—as a money-making factory. Typical areas of pursuit are:

1. *Writing.* Write articles, books, courses, reports, instructions, or ads to mention only a few.

2. *Public Relations.* Develop and provide contact with government officials, influential people, and the general public for a business entity or an association.

3. *Drawing and Painting.* Exploit your drawing and painting capability through commissions and speculation. Or do commercial art, greetings, or advertising art.

4. *Interior Decorating.* Exploit these creative talents by selling your services to one or a group of furnishers. Or sell your services to a user and collect commissions on materials and furnishings purchased.

5. *Sculpture.* See 3 above.

6. *Architecture.* Design buildings and improvements for builders and buyers. Sell your services to local governments. Start a "house plan" service.

7. *Machine Design.* Sell your services to machine manufacturers. Publicize your design capability with articles in trade periodicals.

8. *Product Design.* Sell your services to manufacturers. Watch for new companies and an opportunity to establish a perpetual income through a royalty arrangement or an equity position.

9. *Clothing Design.* See 8 above. In the case of women's dresses, you might hit the jackpot by doing "exclusives" for selected patrons.

10. *Venture Formation.* Develop new ventures by putting ideas, business know-how, and capital together in a profit-making combination.

This list is by no means all-inclusive. If none of these pursuits hits you right between the eyes, perhaps the list will help you discover an ideal situation.

11

HOW TO ORGANIZE, FINANCE, CONTROL, AND OPERATE BIG-PROFIT VENTURES

In this chapter we get down to the nuts and bolts of setting up and running an organization for any of the numerous businesses that we've talked about. We will concern ourselves with organizational form, the pros and cons of organizational form and the technicalities of financing larger ventures. You'll have to translate the discussion to the specific business that you're most interested in.

ORGANIZATIONAL CONSIDERATIONS

In the textbook it's common to encounter discussions concerning proprietorships, partnerships, and corporations, but the discussions are usually nebulous and leave you without a real feel for the best way to go. Actually, the form of organization that you adopt is dictated by the specific aspects of your particular situation. Generally speaking, you'll do well to counsel with your accountant and lawyer before you set up any kind of organizational entity.

I'd like to precede further discussion of organizational structure with some talk about income taxes. First of all, the traditional advice that you receive from most accountants emphasizes the exploitation of the tax laws by deferring taxes and taking the highest possible deductions at the earliest possible time. You'll generally be advised to trade whenever possible, to expense as much as possible, to use double-declining depreciation on new structures and 150 percent declining on used structures. I do not agree with this completely. The reason is that my income will be more substantial in future years. Furthermore, income taxes tend to increase with time. Taxes were reduced during the Kennedy administration, but the general trend over the years has been upward. The institution of the surtax in 1968 has continued this upward trend in taxes. However, the advantage of freeing cash now by taking all expenses as early as possible and by depreciating property as rapidly as possible is a benefit worth considering.

Unless you declare and organize your business in any other form, it is considered a proprietorship. You own full interest in the business, and you alone are responsible for operating it profitably and discharging its obligations. This form of organization tends to make you resource-limited to your own resources. Consequently, if you're starting a proprietorship and have only a small amount of equity capital for your business, you have limitations in the volume of business that you can do. In spite of this, there's a lot to be said for the proprietorship. You're your own boss, and you save a lot of time otherwise lost discussing and getting concurrence from others on the operation of the business. On the other hand, you may penalize yourself by the limited mental and physical resources that one individual can apply in a business. However, one proprietor can do better than a pair of mismatched partners.

The proprietorship and the partnership enjoy tax advantages until the income of the business reaches a relatively high level. Therefore, until such time as the net income of a business begins to put business into the 50 percent tax bracket, there are definite advantages in operating as a proprietorship or as a partnership.

Proprietorships and partnerships involve personal financial responsibilities. Hence if the business fails, the proprietor or partners can be held personally responsible to fulfill financial obligations. I don't see this as a situation to be particularly avoided by any man who is on the up and up. There is a danger, however, in that a partner who loses his sense of moral values or who is incompetent can make agreements or perform acts for which his partner is liable. Since people are very human and subject to physical and mental change, the best partnership in the world can go sour. If it ever happens to you, you may wish you' had a corporation.

The corporation has limited financial responsibilities and, in general, its stockholders are free of personal financial responsibility. Even this has been challenged in recent court cases instituted against the officers and directors of companies.

The corporation possesses another important advantage. It can sell stock (and hence equity) to obtain capital. There is no debt responsibility nor a need to furnish collateral to a stockholder. The stockholder is venturing with you. If your corporation makes out, so does your stockholder; if it falls flat, he loses his investment.

WHEN TO USE A PROPRIETORSHIP

Use a sole proprietorship to get started and also while your business is small. It's easy to form and start. You don't waste time making decisions and you can take swift positive action. As a sole proprietor, you can do almost anything you want to do. You're subject to *no* restrictions, partnership agreements, or corporate charters. The tax advantages are favorable to the proprietorship if the volume of business is small. Record keeping, administration, and operation of the proprietorship are simple.

The disadvantages of a sole proprietorship are that resources are limited and your liability is unlimited. Your financial resources are limited to your cash and borrowing power. You are limited in the amount of management time you have available, and you're limited to your own managerial skill.

THE PROS AND CONS OF PARTNERSHIPS

A partnership is easier to form than a corporation. There are no charter limitations beyond those in the partnership contract. You multiply your resources—capital, borrowing power, management time, management talents, and possibly the synergistics of complementing partner talents.

The disadvantages of a partnership are that one partner may act for the other (or others), one partner may render the other (others) liable, partnership interests are not readily marketable (like stock), and partnerships cannot readily be dissolved when conflict occurs. The personal liability of each partner is unlimited!

Personal liability may be limited through the use of a limited partnership. In this case, you must notify those who extend credit, of the limitations. The corporation is a preferable form of organization when more than one person has equity in a company.

THE PROS AND CONS OF INCORPORATION

The liability of a corporation is generally limited; there are exceptions. The limitation is equal to the amount of stock issued. Equity in the corporation is easy to transfer, and hence the life of a corporation can theoretically be infinite. These features make it possible to attract investors, and hence equity capital. The resources that can be brought into a corporation are unlimited. The corporate form of organization simplifies the mechanics of growth through merger and acquisition and provides a wide choice of alternatives for "making the deal."

The disadvantages of a corporation are additional administrative burden in the form of reports and compliance to regulations, regulation itself, the expense of incorporation, charter limitations, and possible tax disadvantages. The expense of underwriting in going public (if this route is chosen) can be substantial.

HOW TO FORM A CORPORATION

The formation of a corporation is not as complicated as most people believe it to be. While I'm going to discuss how it's done and some of the things that must be considered, you'll still ultimately have to use the services of a lawyer to get the job done. It will cost anything from $100 to $1,000 to form a corporation. In most states, you can do it for less than $500. That includes all fees. There are several choices in the type and form a corporation takes. Your lawyer can advise you on this.

Choose a lawyer who has some corporation experience to help you set up your corporation. While almost any lawyer can do the job, a lawyer who has a good feel for starting corporations, how they work, and how they're financed will be more likely to set it up properly at the outset. An accountant with corporation experience will also make a valuable contribution to the setup operation.

Now, let's get down to the mechanics:

1. You, as the promoter, prepare a chart presentation which outlines your concept of the corporation and its charter. Include the background on the invention, products, and/or form of business, special advantages that apply to the concept, and your contribution to the effort. Show the sales potential and your concept for the growth of the corporation.

2. Develop the deal. How many shares of capital stock will be

authorized? How many shares are to be issued the initial investors? How many shares will you get for conceiving and promoting the organization? What stock will you issue to an inventor and key executive? How long will you need to get all of the investors into the deal?

3. Using the information developed in no. 2 above, draft a preliminary "Agreement to Organize a Corporation." Work the salient features of this mechanism into your chart presentation.

4. Meet with your lawyer. Make your chart presentation to him and show him your preliminary agreement to organize. From this start, he can advise you of changes that you should make and factors that you've overlooked. He'll develop your preliminary agreement to incorporate, into a smooth tentative agreement, and he'll prepare a draft of the "Articles of Incorporation." Ask him to prepare a disclosure form for signature by parties to whom you present your proposition. This protects your ideas.

5. Polish up your chart presentation, and use it to get investors in your company.

6. When your stock has been placed, your lawyer proceeds with the certificate of incorporation, sets up minute books, develops tentative bylaws, and goes through other essential steps.

7. Hold the first meeting of the incorporators. Elect a board of directors and a chairman. Call for payment of the stock subscriptions, and authorize the issuance of stock to the subscribers. Adopt bylaws and handle other matters which your legal counsel and yourself feel to be pertinent. Keep minutes of the proceedings.

The subjects of corporation formation and venture mechanics are multi-faceted and too complex for thorough treatment in this chapter. The order in which some of the mechanics are handled varies from state to state. But, with this knowledge as a base, you'll be able to approach the formation of a corporation more intelligently, and you'll be able to derive the best service from your relationship with your lawyer.

HOW TO GET OFF THE GROUND WITH A JOINT VENTURE OR SYNDICATE

A joint venture is a temporary teaming of individuals and/or companies to pursue specific business objectives. This arrangement develops synergistic benefits. It allows the team to pursue larger deals and objectives, and pools the resources of the participants. Since the arrangement is temporary, the benefits of image building that accrue to a business entity cannot be fully exploited.

A syndicate is similar to a joint venture except that it is usually a longer term proposition. The syndicate is a common organization form in real estate ventures.

Promote your joint venture or syndicate in the same manner as you'd promote a corporation. You mustn't incorporate, but you may be subject to corporation tax.

> *Moonlight Fortune Tip (MFT) 38*
> A proprietorship provides the simplest kind of organization, but tends to be resource limited. A partnership expands resource potential but can lead to difficult situations. A corporation expands resource potential and theoretically has infinite life potential.

SMART DEBT FINANCING

Consider these sources of loans and collateral for loans: life insurance policies, bank-account passbook loans, relatives, friends, specialized agencies.

Here's a way to get collateral if you don't have it: Rent stock. You can rent stock that is traded on the national exchanges from a friend at say 1 to 5 percent. You take this stock and use it as collateral for your loan. This mechanism is particularly good to use with relatives rather than your becoming involved with using the relative's money. Simply rent some of the relative's assets to use as collateral.

If you know that you are going to need money at some time in the future and that some major change is going to occur concerning your location, your place of employment, or your employment, or if you are contemplating going into business, it is wise to borrow the money now. A banker would be reluctant to lend money to you if he knew you were moving out of town or quitting a good-paying job to start your own business. So borrow it now while your situation is extremely stable.

If you live in an area where the interest rate on money is low and are moving to an area where it is higher, borrow the money before you move. If you can borrow at lower interest in a town of former residence, go there to borrow.

SHOP FOR YOUR MONEY

Whenever you have an occasion to borrow money, shop around. Determine whether the interest rate is being charged on the total amount borrowed for the full term or whether it is being charged on the basis of simple interest. For example, if the interest is charged on the total term of the loan, and if the debt is repaid in equal installments, then you're actually paying double the interest rate that is being used. You'll find some difference, too, in the type of loan that you are talking about. For example, with a reasonable credit rating, you can borrow from Texas banks on a term note at simple interest. Hence, on a 90-day note, you might borrow for business purposes at 7½ percent simple interest. Generally you can make arrangements with the bank for paying off a portion of the principal when the note comes due and then getting a new 90-day note for the reduced principal. This process can continue for a period of roughly up to two years, and in some localities, longer. On the other hand, if you are getting an automobile loan, it is probable that the bank will want a higher interest rate. They will work with you on this same term basis, but if you want to pay on a monthly basis, they will lend you the money at 6 percent on the total amount of the loan. Hence, you'll actually be paying 12 percent simple interest. The practice varies from bank to bank and from location to location. But the shrewd million-dollar moonlighter does a little shopping and learns the ins and outs of borrowing and lending before he commits himself.

HOW TO PASS THE BANKER'S TEST

Now let's take a look at some of the factors that bankers consider when they're evaluating your capability to repay a loan. One of the first and foremost things, of course, is net worth. If your net worth is substantial, you can usually borrow 10 to 20 percent of your net worth on your signature. Income is another factor. If you hold a good job, and this incidentally is one of the reasons for getting your start while you are moonlighting, it is assumed by the lender that you will not have to use a portion of the principal to repay the loan. This further strengthens your ability to repay and tends to increase the amount that the bank might consider lending. The third factor is the purpose of the loan. A banker will be more willing to make a loan for investment purposes than he will for a pleasure or leisure item. Another factor is the matter of collateral. If your net worth does not justify a loan or if you have already borrowed a substantial amount on an unsecured basis, you'll have to put up collateral. There is some leeway in what banks can do with respect to collateralized loans, but generally speaking, the collateral that you put up has to be sound and it will usually be discounted so that if the loan is not repaid, the bank can convert the collateralized asset into cash without much trouble. The most important factor of all is an established bank connection. If you've built your relationship with a bank over the years, there's almost no limit to your borrowing power.

When you go to the bank, know how much money you are going to ask for, how you are going to use it, and how you intend to repay it. Present your current financial statement. You can get copies of the Federal Reserve financial statement forms at your bank. Use this standard form in making your statement. Make it factual, and it also pays to make it conservative. Bankers are generally conservative, and if they feel that you are, they are more likely to go along with you.

Incidentally, when you're figuring your net worth for borrowing purposes, bear in mind that bankers will have to discount your homestead since they can't touch this if you renege on your loan commitment.

Another source for loans is the credit union at the place where you are employed. Credit union rates are ordinarily low in contrast to other loans, but they are slightly higher than some of the loans that you might be able to obtain at your bank.

There are numerous other sources where loans can be obtained. Look under "loans" in the Yellow Pages. But, be sure you know what the terms and conditions of the loan are before you sign on the dotted line for anyone. The fine print has undone some supposedly smart people.

> *Moonlight Fortune Tip (MFT) 39*
> Before you borrow, shop around for best
> rates and longest terms.

WHY EQUITY FINANCING?

When you form a partnership, corporation, joint venture, syndicate, or stock company, you release a part of the business equity to other investors. Ideally, you'd like to retain full equity and hence full control, responsibility, and simpler administration. But, this limits your resources and denies you some of the benefits of complementing talents. Your only other source of cash financing beyond your own capital is debt financing. Hence, to retain 100 percent equity, you may have to start very small and grow painfully and very slowly.

Equity financing enables you to start bigger, grow faster, and benefit from a larger resource pool. Suppose you develop a new product. It will take $50,000 to get it on the market. You're a technical man. Get a marketing man into the act with you, and form a promotion team. Set up this way:

1. Authorize 100,000 shares.
2. Sell 10,000 shares at $5 each.
3. Take 50,000 shares divided between the promoters.
4. You have 40,000 shares that can be sold later.

Hence, you have a big chunk of the action without any cash investment. You proceed in promoting and forming the corporation as discussed previously.

PICK PEOPLE WHO'LL DO THE JOB

The absentee owner—and this is a role you often play as a million-dollar moonlighter—needs competent, honest, and sensible people to manage his businesses. They handle your money and apply your resources. Hence, they're key. I've discussed how to find them in earlier chapters. Now, let's talk about *what you look for* and *how you minimize risks*.

Honesty and adequate capability to perform the job are essentials. Don't hire anyone that you're suspicious about. Check their backgrounds, or better yet, bond them. If an applicant passes a bonding agent's check, you've reduced risk considerably. Get references from applicants and check them out. Here are some of the questions to ask of the appropriate references:

1. Tell me about him.
2. What do you think of his character?
3. Does he get along with people?

4. Why did he leave your company?
5. Can he work without supervision?
6. What did he do when he worked for you?
7. How long have you known him?
8. How long did he work for your company?
9. Does he have any bad habits?
10. Do you recommend him?

If his background is negative, the reference may not say so, but you may detect hesitations, tones, and implications that tip you off. Remember, if he's moonlighting for you, don't go back to his full-time employer.

Experience may or may not be important. It depends on the job. I employ inexperienced apartment managers but insist on experienced people in most of my other operations. Attitudes are usually more important than experience. If a fellow's attitudes are right and you train him properly, he may outshine the guy with experience 5 to 1! When you need expertise and specialized advice, it's another story.

> *Moonlight Fortune Tip (MFT) 40*
> Ask job applicants for references and check them out. Bond employees who handle significant amounts of money.

You'll require these specialized talents:

1. Tax and Accounting Counsel
2. Legal Counsel
3. Technical Advisors
4. Other Specialists

Your accountant and your lawyer should be swingers. They should have a wide range of experience in both big and small business activities and problems. You'll limit your growth if you don't choose them with growth and expansion in mind. Both of them should have experience up to the $50-million-a-year corporation level. Otherwise, they might tend to keep you in the little leagues.

Technical advisors should be numerous, with breadth and depth in specialized fields. You can afford to have plenty of them, since you only pay for services you use. Why not pay a little more and get greater depth even if it means dealing with more people?

> *Moonlight Fortune Tip (MFT) 41*
> Hook up with specialists who understand
> special fields in depth. Get with the swingers!

CONTROL AVOIDS LOSSES

Your first control is to try your darndest to pick the right people. Next, you make your procedures and reporting automatic and foolproof. Finally, you meet with your manager periodically—at least once a month, and in some instances at least once a week—at the location of the business, preferably during business hours. That way you see how things are actually being run.

You make your procedures and reporting automatic by using the techniques for record keeping presented in Chapter 1. Forms similar to those shown in Chapter 1, especially tailored to the business in question, will simplify the process. (I mimeograph my own and recommend the acquisition of a mimeograph or spirit duplicator machine if you're really a serious moonlighter.) Periodic inventory is in order if the business carries an inventory of products for sale.

> *Moonlight Fortune Tip (MFT) 42*
> Ben Franklin invented this one: Cut ex-
> penses and control them! "A penny saved
> is a penny earned."

MOTIVATION

Motivation of managers is a key factor in getting successful results as an absentee owner. Money is not a motivator in itself. But if it's applied in a result-oriented incentive program, the achievement motivator goes to work for you in a big way.

Here's the scheme I generally employ with managers:

1. I determine the break-even point—let's assume it's $10,000 sales a month.

2. I pay a small percentage to break even—say 3 percent.

3. I pay a higher percentage on all sales over break-even. It may be 5 to 20 percent depending on the potential. Sometimes I use multiple step escalations.

Hence, my managers really make out when I make good profits. The incentive is geared to the results.

> *Moonlight Fortune Tip (MFT) 43*
> Motivate your managers with incentive pay
> geared to results. Hit the paychecks a good
> lick when break-even is passed and sales
> surge to profit levels.

Don't try to do your manager's work for him. Let him figure some things out for himself. Ask for his suggestions; let him *participate* in steering the business.

A good example goes a long way in motivating people. If your people respect you, they'll usually do a bang-up job for you and try to live by your pattern.

Expand your management know-how with some serious study. My book, *Parametrics, New Key To Successful Take-Charge Management*,[1] covers a broad array of management problems and situations.

BIG MONEY-MAKERS GET 50 TO 1000 PERCENT ANNUAL RETURN

Big money-makers get 50 to 1000 percent annual return on cash invested. Here, compacted into a neat list, is how they do it:

1. They buy right.

2. They use loan leverage.

---

[1] Published by Parker Publishing Co., Inc., West Nyack, N.Y., 1968.

3. They cut expenses to the bone.

4. They divide and recombine assets for top yields.

5. They convert intangibles into cash.

6. They exploit subsidies, government loans, legislation, and regulation.

7. They create deals which satisfy wants and needs of others at a profit.

8. They are constantly on the lookout for special situations.

9. They prefer, seek, and implement perpetual income ventures.

10. They avoid senseless risks but bet fearlessly on sound, nearly sure new ventures.

11. They utilize counsel and expertise to save and make money.

12. They use kickers and motivators on deals and with people.

13. They make fast turnovers and pyramid at the micro level and shoot for perpetual growth at the macro level.

14. They know and use the magic of words and sales expertise.

15. They're sensitive to a changing world—social, economic, technological—in fact, on every frontier.

16. They enter every endeavor with faith, determination, dedicated effort, and a well-laid plan for positive results.

17. They create their own destiny; they accept responsibility for the success or failure of their ventures.

This list is quite compact, but it contains volumes of thoughts on fast wealth building. Read it over again and list the implications and the ideas that each of these items triggers. The exercise should be a beneficial one. It may provide the secret ingredient that will help you put everything you've studied in this book into a neat package with your resources. Possible result: the beginning of your own million-dollar empire. Chapter 12 presents seven case histories of others who did it.

12

MOONLIGHT FORTUNES—
SEVEN ACTUAL CASE HISTORIES—
AND A LOOK AT THE FUTURE

By now you should have a powerful array of money-making techniques under your belt. In this chapter, you'll see how others have used these same techniques to build big fortunes fast.

GLEN HENRY—CAREER MOONLIGHTER

Glen Henry is 48 years old. He has a job with a power company that pays $10,000 a year. He has an interest and working arrangement with a chemical company that earns about $20,000 a year in moonlight income, and he has a used commercial-fixture business that nets him between $10,000 and $20,000 a year. His stock portfolio is probably worth $200,000. His net worth exceeds $1 million.

Glen Henry is not a college graduate. He began his career as a helper in a large corporation's research laboratory. He learned fast, and after three years was moonlighting as a soap manufacturer. He built his moonlight business slowly but surely. When he built it to the point where it demanded full time, he quit his job and moved into the soap business full speed.

Moonlighters often have a hard time settling down to a full-time pursuit of their moonlight starts. Glen Henry is this kind of businessman. When he had an opportunity to sell his soap company for some cash, an interest, and a sales contract, he took the deal. Then, he took the job with the power company. At the age of 30, he had an assured lifetime income from the soap business plus the income from the new job with the power company. Many people would have slowed down at this point. Not Glen Henry!

His next venture was the used store- and office-fixture business. His dealings with store owners and managers in his soap sales activities provided the contacts he needed for a portion of his buying and selling. He expanded his purchasing capability by subscribing to a large number of newspapers and scanning the "Fixtures for Sale" ads. He expanded his sales capability by advertising. Word-of-mouth and his contacts do it all now.

You may wonder where he gets the time for all of this activity. Actually, it doesn't take that much time. He does most of his soap selling by phone. He tracks equipment buyers and sellers by phone. He maintains a man to take care of his equipment warehouse, and he has a number of moonlight workers that he can call on.

LAYTON JACOBS AND CLARENCE DEETER: MOONLIGHTING IN PAIRS

Layton Jacobs was a salesman for an electrical equipment wholesaler. Clarence Deeter was a sales engineer for one of the manufacturers who sold Layton's company. They met and became fast friends over the years. As their friendship grew, their discussions leaned increasingly toward the formation of a business. Neither one of them had a substantial nest egg, and every business idea they came up with seemed to demand more capital than they could raise and more risk than they could shoulder.

One day over coffee they decided to start a moonlight manufacturing operation. The product was to be electric light fixtures, and the factory was Layton Jacobs' garage. The management was Layton Jacobs and Clarence Deeter; so was the shop force.

Together, they developed six basic decorative fixture designs. They made five copies of each. Their total investment to this point was $300. They decided to sell outside of their trade area to avoid conflicts of interest, and decided to do their first selling during their vacations. Future selling, they reasoned, could be done by catalog and phone.

Layton got orders for $3,000 worth of fixtures during his vacation. They bought the materials to fill the order on 30-day open accounts. They hired some high school students to assemble the fixtures, and delivered in three weeks for cash. The pair paid about $1500 in labor and material costs, then repaid their original $300 investment and had $1200 in operating capital.

They put $600 into printing and mailing a small catalog. Repeat orders started coming in from the original purchasers. Clarence Deeter took his vacation and began selling in a new area, while Layton supervised production and shipping at night. After four months of operation, sales were about $5,000 a month. They hired a manager to run the business for 40 percent of the net and became absentee owners. The operations, bursting out of two garages, were consolidated in a leased building. The future looks bright for Clarence and Layton who proved that moonlighting in pairs can pay off.

WALLY AND MARY PERSONS: A MOONLIGHTING COUPLE

Wally Persons manages the meat department in a large supermarket. He began his career in food by cooking in the Army. After the war, he took a job as a butcher and within a few years progressed to his present job. His wife, Mary, was a secretary when they married, but she left her job to start their family which became quite large.

They wanted to start a restaurant but couldn't accumulate a sufficient nest egg. They tried to borrow money but couldn't get a loan. Wally and Mary nursed the idea of owning a restaurant for five years, but they couldn't get a start.

One day a friend of Mary's who had remained in the business world took Mary by her building to show her the new offices. The owner of the building, Mr. Clements, had stopped in to check progress on the remodeling. Mary was introduced to him and told him of her desire to have a restaurant. She told of Wally's knowledge of meat and food preparation and how it would help the restaurant operation. Mr. Clements listened with interest. Then he spoke.

"I'll tell you what I'll do, Mrs. Persons. I'll put the restaurant into this building. You and your husband manage it, and I'll split the net profit with you. After three years you can buy it. And the more you make on the three years of operation, the cheaper you can buy it."

The deal was made. Wally guides the purchasing, cuts the meats, and occasionally cooks. He still has his regular job. Mary works almost a full-time schedule in the restaurant. It's hard work, but in three years she'll own a restaurant with a projected annual net profit of better than $15,000 a year!

GEORGE DANT: A $1 MILLION BUSINESS EMPIRE AFTER TWO FAILURES

Failure Number One: In 1960, with a net worth of about $20,000, most of it in homestead, cars, and furniture, George Dant entered the stock market. He played all of his salary savings and potential savings into it (except for failure number two which I'll explain shortly), and lost around $3,000 over a seven-year period. Actually, his losses were as great as $15,000 at one point, but he recouped some of them.

Failure Number Two: The business he started (in 1964) never got off the ground because the demands of his job made it impossible to really expand it. An investment of $10,000 cash and thousands of hours of labor went into the "ice box."

By 1966, his job pressures had eased and he had some evenings and weekends for moonlight exploration again. His intensive fortune building study, begun in 1964, started anew. He began selling moonlight services that helped him earn some base, and he retrieved some cash by selling out of the market in 1967. If this book had been available to George Dant in 1960, he'd be a millionaire today. Unfortunately it took him seven years and $13,000 to learn it the hard way.

In June of 1967, he began to put his expensive education to work. One year later, his net worth had jumped from around $50,000 to more than $100,000. By January, 1969, his net worth exceeded $150,000 and he controlled $400,000 worth of income-producing assets. He projects a gross income of $75,000 to $100,000 from his moonlight ventures in 1969. He'll pull no cash because he'll pour his net into debt service and new "smart buy" investments. By the end of 1969 he projects control of $750,000 in assets, and by the end of 1970 he projects $1.3 million in controlled assets.

Hence, in three years, George Dant will have pyramided about $10,000 into a $1.3-million-dollar empire! He invests in a diversified array of properties, several small retail operations, and a number of minor inventions. George started by buying equities in houses, taking his cash flow to buy more, and then diversifying into retail businesses. He finds good managers and gives them 50 percent of the net profits. Every one is a money-maker.

HARRY BLACKMAN: FROM $1,000 CASH TO $100,000 EQUITY IN ONE YEAR

George Dant builds perpetual money-making machines. Harry Blackman is a trader. He started by buying an equity in a $15,000 house for $500. He fixed it up for another $500, and traded his equity in the house for equity in an eight-unit apartment. His net worth jumped about $12,000 on the deal. The apartment was run-down, so he refinanced for $20,000 above the existing debt. He got $12,000 cash immediately with $8,000 held in escrow pending fix-up.

Harry did the fix-up for $2,000, got the other $8,000, and proceeded to trade his equity for a run-down antique shop in an old (but title-clear) house. He paid $5,000 cash for the antique-shop inventory. Blackman sold out the top-value items to department stores for window displays and pulled $15,000. He refurbished the house, organized the antique shop on the bottom floor, put two apartments upstairs and gave the antique shop a big publicity push.

He did this whole thing as a moonlighter using hired help and his business contacts. Only 13 months after he started, he traded the antique shop for a small manufacturing business. His moonlight equity had grown to $100,000 plus!

Harry Blackman is having some problems with the manufacturing business at this time. He believes that perhaps it doesn't fit him. He's just hired a team of (moonlight) manufacturing experts to help him solve the problems. When he turns the trick, he intends to sell the manufacturing company and set up a savings and loan association.

MILES KAUFFMANN: $200 TO $50,000 IN ONE YEAR— WITH THE HELP OF CHANCE

Miles Kauffmann was a production worker nearing retirement. One Saturday afternoon he was meandering around downtown Fort Worth, Texas, passing the time aimlessly. He noticed an old hotel building with a sign in the window that said: Furnishings for Sale, Place Bids in Box.

He tried the door. It was open. He walked in and began to nose around. He decided to bid on the furnishings "just for the hell of it."

Monday morning at 5:30 A.M. he received a phone call.

"Your bid was high. You'll have to get everything out of the building by midnight Wednesday as indicated in the bid instructions." Miles called in to work and made arrangements for one of the night-shift men to work his day for him. Then he got busy rounding up trucks, renting an old house, and getting everything coordinated. After all,

    70 Brass Beds
    20 Victorian Easy Chairs
    10 Victorian Sofas
    80 Tiffany Lamp Shades
    80 Oak Dressers
  200 Wooden Chairs
    60 Mattress and Spring Sets
    And about 500 Other Items—

take a while to move.

At nine o'clock, Miles walked into the office of a property investment company, paid the $200 he had bid, and began to move his plunder out—$50,000 dollars' worth of it! During the next year he sold nearly every item he had bought, and launched an antique business that earns ten times his salary. Miles Kauffmann saw an opportunity and seized it!

BILL LOFTON: $1,000 TO $1 MILLION—IN THREE YEARS

Bill Lofton is a technical man. He was a $12,000-a-year engineer who started to develop a piece of peripheral computer equipment in his garage. After a year of moonlight work and a cash investment of about $1,000, he had two working prototypes and a U.S. patent application.

At this point, he sought investors, and lined up a lawyer, a doctor, and a professional investor who put down $50,000, plus a $50,000 line of credit for 60 percent of the company that was formed. He went into production, and his business boomed. His $1,000 investment became a million-dollar equity in three years.

Bill Lofton owes a large portion of his success to his technical know-how. But, a far larger factor in his success was the knowledge and application of the techniques and skills presented in this book—especially the business principles of Chapter 11. His technical knowledge got him started. His moonlighting knowledge and skill carried him through and made his success a big one!

COMPELLING SECRETS BEHIND THE MONEY-MAKERS

Money-makers are a breed apart. They need not be highly educated or polished. Nor need they be versed in the ways of the drawing room, the statehouse, the golf course, the theater, the church, or the manners of the society ball. They need not be gentle. Nor do they need the polished speech of the professional lecturer or the radio commentator. Yet, the money-maker who has these things (most money-makers acquire them) fares just a little better than some of those who never do acquire these graces.

The most outstanding attribute of the successful money-maker and fortune builder is the glint in his eye, the joy in his heart, when he sees an opportunity to render a service at a profit. He has enthusiasm for the deal, zest for the effort, and he feels excitement in the profit.

Next to his love of the pursuit of wealth, the natural money-maker is a persistent, no-quit pusher who keeps going after what he wants. If he can't make a deal going in one direction, he tries another. The successful money-maker never states the terms of any deal with finality. He always leaves room to move back in with a counter-offer in case the first one is rejected.

Another characteristic of the fortune builder is his constant scanning for opportunities. His eyes, his ears, and his mind sweep the horizon and its surroundings like an all-seeing radar. He scans the want ads, listens to conversations, reads technical and trade periodicals. He frequents his library, talks to others and finds ideas and opportunities everywhere. The world is his workshop. He reclaims marshes and builds skyscrapers on them. He buys squalid buildings and converts them into luxury apartments. Since the days of Marco Polo, he has brought spices from the Orient, precision machines from Europe, ivory from Africa, coffee from South America, and even more wonderful products from the laboratory.

Fortune builders are willing to take a chance. The investments with the big returns always have the bigger risks. Safe investments usually have lower returns. So, the big fortune builder pursues the riskier situations with a higher possible return. The no-risk fortune builder hedges his risks and always keeps a few "sure things" going.

The astute money-maker is willing to share profits. He shares profits to obtain equity financing. He shares profits to get special talents. He frequently shares profits with a partner because when two are running an enterprise, one keeps running and pulling whenever the other one tends to rest.

The wealth-oriented individual is not afraid to sign his name on a big note. He is always willing to borrow as much money as he can, but never for pleasure or other personal use. He borrows it to invest and to make additional money. He enjoys the money that he makes after he has made it, never before.

The real money-maker is a dreamer of sorts. He's always investing his future profits, but his dreams are really more than that. They are exercises that lead to concrete plans with alternatives and future modes of profitable departure when his current projects yield profits, and hence, new capital.

The fortune builder is sometimes very decisive—often very deliberate. He analyzes each business situation that he enters in as much detail as he must. If a deal is similar to one he has entered into before, he devotes less time to it than he devotes to analyzing a new, unfamiliar deal. In other words, when he feels that he knows his business, he moves ahead confidently and rapidly. If he's in an area where he does not feel so expert, he takes his time to come up with correct decisions.

Most wealth builders are money smart. They may not be highly degreed, perhaps not even educated beyond grade school, but when it comes to matters of money and the businesses that they engage in, they are expert. They get that way by studying, by observing, and through experience.

Some wealth builders are incremental wealth builders, while others are plungers. The incremental wealth builder makes a small investment and reaps a high-percentage profit. Although his profit is not as great as if more had been invested, he can, through a number of deals, make as much money as if he had invested much in one deal. If some of his deals turn sour, he is always assured of a profit from the deals that are successful. The plunger, on the other hand, makes bigger killings on each deal that he makes; but if one goes sour, his loss is sometimes substantial and perhaps even catastrophic. Use whichever way you feel is best for you.

Some wealth builders don't start with money; they start only with their mind. They work on the principle that their mind is a bottomless treasure chest filled with ideas that can be extracted and converted into cash. Typical of this group of wealth builders are writers, inventors, composers, lecturers, teachers, and consultants.

Still another group of wealth builders who do not use money use skill. These skills are sometimes less creative than the skills of the "idea-seller," but they are skills for rendering services to other people. Typical professional and skilled profit-makers are doctors, dentists, lawyers, engineers, manufacturing specialists, repairmen, plumbers, carpenters, and others.

No matter what your background may be, you can join the moonlight fortune club. Study this book. Supplement your study with the references I cited and other references that you'll discover in the pursuit of this fortune building adventure. Discuss business and investment matters with others who are knowledgeable in their fields. Then, get started in the actual business of making money. Before you know it, your financial status will exceed your wildest dreams.

A LOOK AT THE FUTURE

There'll be a lot of changes in the 1970–1980 decade. By 1980, you'll be ten years older, and if you harness the rocket to moonlight riches, far wealthier. Here's what you can expect in 1980:

1. *Population* was 180 million in 1960, will reach 205 million in 1970 and an estimated 235 to 245 million in 1980.

2. *GNP* was $504 billion in 1960, and will reach the $1 trillion mark in 1970; $1.5 trillion in 1980.

3. *Computer Technology* will institute new ways of doing business. Checking accounts will be controlled with coded cards —you won't write checks.

4. *Pollution Control* will grow by leaps and bounds as man seeks to control the fouling of his nest. The external combustion engine with Freon, steam or some other working fluid will replace the explosive, air-fouling internal combustion engine. This move is important because about 95 percent of all prime mover horsepower generated is for automotive use.

5. *Automation and Controls* will cause drastic changes in industry, the work week, and the service industry. New control systems will reduce loss of life by accident in autos, homes, industry, and by fire.

6. *Construction Technology,* reacting to the pressures for homes at lower cost in an inflating materials and labor market, will produce lower cost factory-made modules. The promoters and manufacturers will reap vast new fortunes.

7. *Education and Educational Technology* will grow by

leaps and bounds. We're now spending in excess of $70 billion a year in this area. By 1980, the tab will rise to $100–$150 billion. The synergistic effects of education and the equal-opportunity push will give this field fantastic impetus.

8. *Waste Disposal and Salvage* will become an industry ranking in the top five. Garbage disposal and attendant costs are already plaguing large American cities—freight trains daily carry hundreds of tons of garbage hundreds of miles for disposal. Furthermore, salvage of usable products and materials is a must to avoid exhaustion of our known resources.

9. *Service Technology* must advance to meet demand. Smart scientific minds will compete with the clumsy, overcharging manual servicemen to provide scientific diagnosis and repair at lower cost.

10. *Medical Technology* will advance to prolong life and make the terminal years more pleasant. New industries will spring up to cater to the 65 to 110 age group. It's already started.

11. *Work Week* in 1980 will be 35 hours for most Americans. Only million-dollar moonlighters will work longer. But moonlighting will increase. To meet the crisis of individual entrepreneurship, big business will increase the scope of stock-option plans and other incentive programs.

12. *Hippyism, Rioting, and Protest* of the late '60's will be assaulted by the counteraction of the middle-income group ($15,000 to $25,000) by 1980. They'll assault by holding their money back, exerting pressure on politicians, and by resorting to the kind of force that the irresponsible are "teaching" them today. Look for vigilante committees if the government can't cope with it.

HERE'S HOW YOU CAN DO IT

Get the principles presented in this book under your belt. Start to build your information and push toward a definite series of plans. Then start playing the game with real money.

I don't want to review and repeat here what I've presented in this book. *It's your job to go back through the book and establish these principles firmly in your mind. It's your job to find your own bag!* No one can advise you which road you'll travel most successfully to your own million-dollar empire. Others can show you some of the roads and they can show you some of the mechanics of making the journey. But *you* have to make the trip. It starts with the *first step—everything leading to the first collection of money* for investment and effort. Between that step and the chair at the helm of the million-dollar business empire, there'll be some hard work, trauma, and a few falls. But the chair and the empire are there, waiting for you to earn and claim them.

Young Man: How did you get rich?
Rich Man: By making the right decisions.
Young Man: How did you make the right decisions?
Rich Man: By applying experience.
Young Man: How did you get experience?
Rich Man: By making the wrong decisions.